OnCourse

The U.S. Ski & Snowboard
Teams' Cookbook

Library of Congress Number: 97-060651
ISBN: 9656950-0-X

Designed, Edited and Manufactured by
Favorite Recipes® Press
an imprint of

FRP™

P.O. Box 305142, Nashville, Tennessee 37230
800-358-0560

Cover and Book Design: Bill Kersey

Manufactured in the United States of America
First Printing: 1997 10,000 copies

Contents

Preface

The U.S. Ski Team Foundation is the nonprofit fund-raising arm of the U.S. Ski and Snowboard Team. The organization represents seven snow sport disciplines: Alpine, Cross Country, Disabled, Freestyle, Jumping, Nordic Combined, and Snowboarding. The proceeds from *On Course: The U.S. Ski & Snowboard Teams' Cookbook* directly benefit the competition, athlete training, development, and educational needs of U.S. Ski Team and U.S. Snowboard Team athletes. The United States teams receive no federal funding and operate solely through individual and corporate contributions. Your purchase of this cookbook truly helps our U.S. athletes toward their American dream.

Introduction

*O*n Course: The U.S. Ski & Snowboard Teams' Cookbook is a collection of favorite recipes coupled with favorite moments from the U.S. Ski and Snowboard Teams' long and interesting history. Each page delivers tasty recipes and fun facts about the legends of United States skiing and snowboarding.

The recipes included here represent favorite or classic recipes and in no way reflect the nutritional guidelines recommended for elite U.S. Team athletes.

We're glad you've chosen to share a moment with the U.S. Ski Team Foundation. We hope you enjoy being On Course with all of our favorites!

Contributors

Janine Alfano	*Tom Kelly*	*Ron Shepard*
Luke Bodensteiner	*Genevieve Kiley*	*Trisha Skalicky*
Tina Bowers	*Bill Marolt*	*Picabo Street*
Todd Burnette	*Connie Marolt*	*Tiffany Timmons*
Steve Johnson	*Paul Robbins*	*Trace Worthington*

Photo Credits

Front Cover
Todd Lodwick
photo by Tim Hancock, SportsFile

Page 39
Sarah Billmeier
photo by Christian Schneider

Back Cover
Picabo Street and Hilary Lindh
photo by Tim Hancock, SportsFile

Page 55
Trace Worthington
photo by Mark Maziarz

Page 9
Matt Grosjean
USSA photo by Nathan Bilow

Page 73
Tim Tetreault
USSA photo by Nathan Bilow

Page 23
U.S. Cross Country Ski Team
USSA photo by Nathan Bilow

Page 89
Marcus Nash
USSA photo by Nathan Bilow

Page 105
Sandra VanErt
USSA photo by Nathan Bilow

Nutritional Profile Guidelines

The editors have attempted to present these recipes in a form that allows approximate nutritional values to be computed. Persons with dietary or health problems or whose diets require close monitoring should not rely solely on the nutritional information provided. They should consult their physicians or a registered dietitian for specific information.

Abbreviations for Nutritional Profiles

Cal – Calories	T Fat – Total Fat	Sod – Sodium
Prot – Protein	Chol – Cholesterol	g – grams
Carbo – Carbohydrates	Fiber – Dietary Fiber	mg – milligrams

Nutritional information for these recipes is computed from information derived from many sources, including materials supplied by the United States Department of Agriculture, computer databanks, and journals in which the information is assumed to be in the public domain. However, many specialty items, new products, and processed foods may not be available from these sources or may vary from the average values used in these profiles. More information on new and/or specific products may be obtained by reading the nutrient labels. Unless otherwise specified, the nutritional profiles of these recipes are based on all measurements being level.

- **Artificial sweeteners** vary in use and strength so should be used "to taste," using the recipe ingredients as a guideline. Sweeteners using aspartame (NutraSweet and Equal) should not be used as a sweetener in recipes involving prolonged heating, which reduces the sweet taste. For further information on the use of these sweeteners, refer to the package.
- **Alcoholic ingredients** have been analyzed for the basic ingredients, although cooking causes the evaporation of alcohol, thus decreasing caloric content.
- **Buttermilk, sour cream,** and **yogurt** are the types available commercially.
- **Cake mixes** which are prepared using package directions include 3 eggs and $^1/_2$ cup oil.
- **Chicken,** cooked for boning and chopping, has been roasted; this method yields the lowest caloric values.
- **Cottage cheese** is cream-style with 4.2% creaming mixture. Dry curd cottage cheese has no creaming mixture.
- **Eggs** are all large. To avoid raw eggs that may carry salmonella as in eggnog or 6-week muffin batter, use an equivalent amount of commercial egg substitute.
- **Flour** is unsifted all-purpose flour.
- **Garnishes,** serving suggestions, and other optional additions and variations are not included in the profiles.
- **Margarine** and **butter** are regular, not whipped or presoftened. Milk is whole milk, 3.5% butterfat. Lowfat milk is 1% butterfat. Evaporated milk is whole milk with 60% of the water removed. **Oil** is any vegetable cooking oil. **Shortening** is hydrogenated vegetable shortening.
- **Salt** and other ingredients to taste as noted in the ingredients have not been included in the nutritional profiles.
- If a choice of ingredients has been given, the nutritional profiles reflect the first option. If a choice of amounts has been given, the nutritional profiles reflect the greater amount.
- Refer to a general cooking guide for **high altitude** time, temperature, or ingredient adjustments.

Alpine Skiing

Alpine ski racing is pretty basic: a skier goes down a snowy mountainside from Point A to Point B and the fastest time wins. No judging, just go! Races are timed in hundredths of a second.

There are four types of races: slalom, giant slalom (GS), super G, and downhill (DH). Downhill is the high-speed attention-getter with racers rocketing along at speeds up to 80 miles an hour in some stretches, while slalom has a zig-zag staccato tempo. In between are GS and super G. DH and super G are one-run races; slalom and giant slalom are two-run events.

Part of the beauty is the beat-the-clock simplicity. The one rule is "Get to the bottom fastest." Style and grace are less factors than the pulsating "on the edge" quality of screaming down a mountainside.

Downhill and super G are known as "speed" events for obvious reasons: racers generate the most speed over a long course (two miles or so in length, up to two minutes of skiing in the longest downhills) with only a few control gates to brake their high-speed descent.

Slalom and GS are "technical" events because they pose a more technical course as racers face more control gates or slalom poles to ski around. Slalom is the opposite of downhill as racers dash helter-skelter around hinged "breakaway" slalom poles, specially designed to bounce down as a skier pushes them out of the way and then spring back into position.

There's also combined, which has a bit of a split personality. On one hand, it's a "paper event," i.e., not competed but calculated based on results from designated races, a downhill and slalom, on the World Cup (and U.S. championships). On the other hand, at the Olympics and World Championships, combined is made up of two actual races (on shorter downhill and slalom courses), forming a fifth alpine "event."

"Skiing is the freedom of the sport. You pick your own path down the hill. It's the mix of speed and turns," said AJ Kitt, a former World Cup downhill winner. "And the speed of the turns can throw your equilibrium off a little bit, making it more fun."

Appetizers

Beefy Bean Dip

1¹/₂ pounds lean ground beef

1 large onion, chopped

Chili powder to taste

Salt to taste

2 (16-ounce) cans kidney beans

3 tablespoons chili powder

¹/₂ cup catsup

2 tablespoons Tabasco sauce

2 cups shredded sharp Cheddar cheese

2 bunches green onions, finely chopped

2 cups sliced green olives

* Brown the ground beef with onion, chili powder to taste and salt in a skillet, stirring frequently; drain.
* Drain 1 can of the kidney beans. Combine the drained beans with the remaining undrained beans, 3 tablespoons chili powder, catsup and Tabasco sauce in a blender container. Process for 2 to 3 minutes or until well blended.
* Layer the ground beef mixture, bean mixture, cheese, green onions and olives in an electric skillet.
* Cook for 15 to 20 minutes or until heated through.
* Serve warm with tortilla chips.

Yield: 25 servings

Approx Per Serving: Cal 154; Prot 10 g; Carbo 8 g; T Fat 10 g;
55% Calories from Fat; Chol 27 mg; Fiber 4 g; Sod 704 mg

Kirk Cutter (Bend, OR) won the first World Cup race won by an American
skier—taking a slalom in Oslo in 1968; victory number 100 went to Hilary Lindh
(Juneau, AK), who won a downhill at Sierra Nevada, Spain, in 1994.

Faux Caviar Dip

2 (16-ounce) cans black-eyed peas, drained
1 (16-ounce) can white hominy, drained
2 medium tomatoes, chopped
3 green onions, chopped
2 jalapeños, chopped
1¹⁄₄ cups chopped onions
1 cup finely chopped parsley
1 clove of garlic, minced
1 (8-ounce) bottle Italian salad dressing

＊ Combine the peas, hominy, tomatoes, green onions, jalapeños, onions, parsley and garlic in a bowl and mix well.
＊ Combine with the salad dressing in a serving bowl and mix well.
＊ Chill in the refrigerator for 2 hours.
＊ Serve with large corn chips.
＊ May process half the pea mixture in a blender for smoother consistency if desired.

Yield: 12 servings

Approx Per Serving: Cal 180; Prot 5 g; Carbo 20 g; T Fat 12 g;
52% Calories from Fat; Chol 0 mg; Fiber 6 g; Sod 432 mg

The first official U.S. national championship was the men's downhill, held March 12, 1933, on
the Carriage Road on Mount Moosilauke (NH). H.S. (Bern) Woods, a Dartmouth skier,
won the title. The first women's U.S. championship, also the downhill, was held on April 9, 1938,
on the fabled Nosedive Trail on Mount Mansfield in Stowe, Vermont, with Marian (Sis) McKean
(Beverly Farms, MA) winning the title.

Low-Fat Chili Dip

3 (16-ounce) cans kidney beans
1¹/₂ pounds ground chuck
1¹/₂ onions, chopped
1¹/₂ green bell peppers, chopped
2¹/₂ (20-ounce) bottles hot catsup
1¹/₂ tablespoons cumin
1¹/₂ tablespoons chili powder

* Drain the kidney beans, reserving the liquid. Mash the kidney beans.
* Brown the ground chuck with the onions and green peppers in a saucepan, stirring until the ground chuck is crumbly; drain.
* Add the kidney beans, reserved liquid, catsup, cumin and chili powder and mix well.
* Simmer for 2 hours, stirring occasionally.
* Garnish with shredded cheese and sliced black olives.

Yield: 50 servings

Approx Per Serving: Cal 86; Prot 5 g; Carbo 13 g; T Fat 2 g;
22% Calories from Fat; Chol 10 mg; Fiber 2 g; Sod 439 mg

Billy Kidd (Stowe, VT), a University of Colorado grad, retired from World Cup racing after winning the gold medal in combined at the 1970 World Alpine Ski Championships in Val Gardena, Italy. He turned professional and won the world pro title a couple of weeks later, making him (still) the only skier to win both "amateur" and pro world championships in the same season.

"As-Hot-as-You-Want-It" Salsa

1 firm white onion, chopped
2 ripe tomatoes, chopped
2 to 4 fresh jalapeños, chopped
Juice of 2 or 3 fresh limes
2 tablespoons cilantro
Olive oil to taste
Salt to taste
1 or 2 ripe avocados, chopped

* Combine the onion, tomatoes, jalapeños and lime juice in a bowl and mix well.
* Stir in the cilantro. Drizzle with olive oil; season with salt.
* Spoon into a large clear glass bowl.
* Stir in the avocados just before serving.
* Will keep in refrigerator for approximately 1 day.

Yield: 4 servings

Approx Per Serving: Cal 199; Prot 0 g; Carbo 16 g; T Fat 16 g;
72% Calories from Fat; Chol 0 mg; Fiber 5 g; Sod 17 mg

Diann Roffe (Williamson, NY) was the first U.S. racer to win a medal at the World
Junior Alpine Championships, taking silver in giant slalom at Maine's Sugarloaf/USA resort
in 1984. A year later, she won the grand slalom title at the World Championships in
Bormio, Italy; a month later, she won her first World Cup race, capturing a grand slalom
at Whiteface Mountain outside Lake Placid, New York.

Hummus with Taratour Sauce

3 cups cooked garbanzo beans
2 cloves of garlic, minced
5 tablespoons fresh lemon juice
Salt to taste
³/₄ cup Taratour Sauce
1 tablespoon olive oil
2 tablespoons chopped parsley

* Purée the garbanzo beans and garlic in a food processor. Add the lemon juice, salt and Taratour Sauce.
* Process to the consistency of mayonnaise, adding water if necessary. Spread in a shallow bowl.
* Sprinkle with the olive oil and parsley.
* Serve with pita bread, Greek olives and pepperoni.

Yield: 6 servings

Approx Per Serving: Cal 292; Prot 10 g; Carbo 33 g; T Fat 15 g;
44% Calories from Fat; Chol 0 mg; Fiber 2 g; Sod 544 mg

Taratour Sauce

¹/₂ cup tahini (sesame seed paste)
1 large clove of garlic, minced
¹/₄ cup fresh lemon juice
¹/₂ teaspoon salt
¹/₄ cup cold water

* Blend the tahini and garlic in a food processor. Add the lemon juice, salt and water.
* Blend to the consistency of thick mayonnaise, adding additional water if necessary.

Gate-Runners' Tabouli

1 cup bulgur

1¹/₂ cups boiling water

1¹/₂ teaspoons salt

¹/₄ cup fresh lemon juice

2 cloves of garlic, minced

¹/₄ cup olive oil

¹/₂ cup chopped green onions

2 tablespoons chopped fresh mint

2 medium tomatoes, diced

1 cup packed chopped parsley

* Combine the bulgur, boiling water and salt in a bowl. Let stand, covered, for 15 to 20 minutes or until the bulgur is softened.
* Add the lemon juice, garlic, olive oil, green onions and mint and mix well.
* Chill for 2 to 3 hours. Add the tomatoes and parsley just before serving and toss gently. Adjust seasonings if desired.
* Garnish with Greek olives and feta cheese.

Yield: 6 servings

Approx Per Serving: Cal 198; Prot 4 g; Carbo 26 g; T Fat 10 g;
42% Calories from Fat; Chol 0 mg; Fiber 7 g; Sod 543 mg

Phil Mahre won the overall alpine World Cup title for three straight seasons, starting in 1981. When he retired after the 1984 season, he had 27 World Cup wins: eight in slalom, eight in giant slalom, eleven in combined, plus an Olympic gold medal (slalom, 1984) and Olympic silver (slalom, 1980).

Hot Crab Salad Canapés

1 (10-ounce) can cream of mushroom soup

¹/₃ cup milk

1 small onion, chopped

3 cups chopped celery

¹/₄ teaspoon seafood seasoning

1 pound crab meat

1¹/₂ tablespoons butter

1¹/₂ tablespoons flour

¹/₄ teaspoon Worcestershire sauce

¹/₂ teaspoon salt

Pepper to taste

³/₄ cup milk

¹/₂ cup shredded Swiss cheese

4 English muffins, cut into halves, toasted

* Combine the soup, ¹/₃ cup milk, onion, celery and seafood seasoning in a saucepan.
* Cook over low heat for 10 minutes, stirring often. Add the crab meat.
* Cook until heated through, stirring gently. Set aside.
* Melt the butter in a heavy saucepan. Remove from the heat. Blend in the flour, Worcestershire sauce, salt and pepper. Stir in ³/₄ cup milk gradually.
* Cook over low heat until thickened, stirring constantly. Cook for 5 minutes longer. Add the cheese, stirring until melted.
* Place the muffins on an ovenproof serving plate. Top each half with the crab meat mixture. Pour the cheese sauce over the top.
* Broil until the cheese sauce is light brown.
* Cut into bite-size pieces.

Yield: 4 servings

Approx Per Serving: Cal 488; Prot 36 g; Carbo 43 g; T Fat 19 g;
36% Calories from Fat; Chol 147 mg; Fiber 4 g; Sod 1746 mg

Burgundy Mushrooms

1 quart burgundy

2 cups butter

1 tablespoon Worcestershire sauce

1 tablespoon garlic powder

2 teaspoons salt

1 teaspoon pepper

3 chicken bouillon cubes

3 beef bouillon cubes

3 vegetable bouillon cubes

1 teaspoon dillweed

2 cups boiling water

10 pounds mushrooms

* Combine the wine, butter, Worcestershire sauce, garlic powder, salt, pepper, bouillon cubes, dillweed and boiling water in a slow cooker.
* Rinse the mushrooms. Add to the wine mixture several at a time, allowing the mushrooms to shrink in size before adding more.
* Simmer, covered, over low heat for 4 hours. Simmer, uncovered, for 4 hours longer.
* Remove the mushrooms with a slotted spoon to a serving bowl.
* May be frozen covered in liquid, adding additional wine if needed.

Yield: 40 servings

Approx Per Serving: Cal 129; Prot 3 g; Carbo 6 g; T Fat 10 g;
71% Calories from Fat; Chol 25 mg; Fiber 2 g; Sod 431 mg

The United States has hosted the World Alpine Ski Championship twice, both

times in Colorado—1950 in Aspen and 1989 in Vail and Beaver Creek. The championships

return to Vail and Beaver Creek in 1999.

Oysters in Champagne Sauce

2 cloves of garlic, thinly sliced

2 tablespoons butter

1 pound small oysters

1 cup dry Champagne

¹/₂ cup whipping cream

1 pound fresh spinach, rinsed

1 tablespoon butter

1 tablespoon flour

Salt to taste

* Sauté the garlic in 2 tablespoons butter in a skillet for several minutes. Add the oyster liquid, Champagne and whipping cream.
* Simmer until reduced by about ¹/₃. Add the oysters. Place the spinach on top.
* Cook, covered, for several minutes; do not overcook the oysters.
* Cook the remaining 1 tablespoon butter and flour in a small skillet for several minutes to make a roux, stirring constantly.
* Remove the spinach to a serving plate and keep warm. Place the oysters on the spinach.
* Add the roux to the pan drippings. Cook until thickened, stirring constantly.
* Pour the sauce over the oysters.
* May serve as a main dish with green salad with pesto vinaigrette, risotto with mushrooms, French rolls and chablis or chardonnay.

Yield: 4 servings

Approx Per Serving: Cal 336; Prot 12 g; Carbo 13 g; T Fat 23 g;
62% Calories from Fat; Chol 126 mg; Fiber 4 g; Sod 303 mg

In 1983, Phil Mahre (White Pass, WA) won the men's alpine World Cup overall title

while Tamara McKinney (Squaw Valley, CA) won the women's overall title. Each of them also

was the World Cup giant slalom champion.

Marinated Shrimp and Artichoke Hearts

15 pounds shrimp

1 package crab boil

6 (16-ounce) cans artichoke hearts, drained

4 onions, sliced

30 bay leaves

10 pounds fresh mushrooms

6 cups vegetable oil

3 cups white vinegar

8 drops (about) of Tabasco sauce

³/₄ cup capers, drained

3 tablespoons celery seeds

2 tablespoons salt

* Cook the shrimp with crab boil in water to cover in a large stockpot until cooked through; drain. Peel and devein the shrimp. Cut large artichoke hearts into halves.
* Layer the shrimp, artichoke hearts, onions, bay leaves and mushrooms in a large bowl.
* Combine the oil, vinegar, Tabasco sauce, capers, celery seeds and salt in a bowl and mix well. Pour over the layers.
* Marinate in the refrigerator for 24 hours.
* Stir to mix well at serving time. Serve with toothpicks.

Yield: 60 servings

Approx Per Serving: Cal 326; Prot 22 g; Carbo 10 g; T Fat 23 g;
63% Calories from Fat; Chol 177 mg; Fiber 2 g; Sod 452 mg
Nutritional information contains entire amount of marinade;
it does not include crab boil or capers.

Bill Johnson (Van Nuys, CA) was the first American man to win a World Cup
downhill, taking the Lauberhorn January 15, 1984, in Wengen, Switzerland. He won two more
World Cup downhills that season (Aspen, Whistler) plus Olympic gold in Sarajevo.

Spinach Pie

¹/₂ pound Italian sausage, cooked

2 (10-ounce) packages frozen chopped spinach, thawed

¹/₄ cup tomato sauce

1 (6-ounce) can sliced mushrooms

¹/₄ cup grated Parmesan cheese

2 loaves frozen bread dough, thawed

1 tablespoon vegetable oil

¹/₄ teaspoon paprika

¹/₄ teaspoon oregano

❋ Combine the sausage, spinach, tomato sauce, mushrooms and Parmesan cheese in a bowl and mix well.

❋ Pat 1 loaf of the bread dough ¹/₂ inch thick on a baking sheet. Spread with the sausage mixture.

❋ Pat the remaining loaf bread dough ¹/₂ inch thick on a floured surface. Place on top of the sausage mixture.

❋ Seal the edges. Rub with the oil. Sprinkle with the paprika and oregano.

❋ Bake at 400 degrees for 25 to 30 minutes or until golden brown and slightly raised in the center.

Yield: 8 servings

Approx Per Serving: Cal 396; Prot 16 g; Carbo 60 g; T Fat 11 g;
24% Calories from Fat; Chol 12 mg; Fiber 5 g; Sod 942 mg

Cindy Nelson (Lutsen, MN) was 20 years old when she won the downhill bronze medal at the 1976 Olympics in Innsbruck, Austria. She competed in four Olympics, starting at Sapporo in 1972, and medaled in four straight major championships: bronze in the 1976 Olympic downhill, bronze in combined at the 1978 Worlds, World Championships silver in combined in 1980 when the Olympics still doubled as World Championships (there was no Olympic combined then), and silver in combined at the 1982 Worlds.

New Potato Appetizers

1/2 cup sour cream

2 tablespoons chopped chives

24 small new potatoes

4 slices bacon, crisp-fried, crumbled

* Mix the sour cream and chives together in a small bowl and set aside.
* Cook the potatoes in boiling water to cover in a saucepan until tender; drain.
* Let the potatoes stand until cool enough to handle easily. Cut into halves; scoop out the centers with a teaspoon or melon baller.
* Fill the potatoes with the sour cream mixture. Sprinkle with the bacon.
* Chill until serving time.
* May add 1/3 teaspoon garlic powder to the sour cream mixture.

Yield: 24 servings

Approx Per Serving: Cal 90; Prot 2 g; Carbo 17 g; T Fat 2 g;
20% Calories from Fat; Chol 3 mg; Fiber 2 g; Sod 25 mg

Spicy Pecans

2 cups sugar

1/2 cup water   2 teaspoons cinnamon

1 teaspoon nutmeg

1/2 teaspoon (or less) cloves

1 1/2 teaspoons salt   4 cups pecan halves

* Combine the sugar, water, cinnamon, nutmeg, cloves and salt in a deep 3-quart glass bowl and mix well.
* Microwave, covered with waxed paper, on High for 4 minutes; mix well.
* Microwave for 2 1/2 to 4 1/2 minutes or to 234 to 240 degrees on a candy thermometer, soft-ball stage.
* Add the pecans, stirring until well coated.
* Spread on waxed paper and separate with a fork. Cool completely.

Yield: 16 servings

Approx Per Serving: Cal 295; Prot 2 g; Carbo 30 g; T Fat 20 g;
61% Calories from Fat; Chol 0 mg; Fiber 2 g; Sod 201 mg

Cross Country Skiing

Cross country is the original and most popular nordic skisport, so named because it originated in northern Europe (as opposed to alpine, which draws its name from the Alps, where downhill skiing became so widespread).

For years, cross country meant one technique, i.e., "diagonal stride" where both skis stayed in prepared tracks. Skiers put "kick" and "glide" waxes on the bottom of each ski; the kick wax was for grip on the uphill sections while the glide wax helped propel the skier through downhill sections and over rolling terrain.

In 1982, American Bill Koch popularized the "skating" technique, a style which had been used in Europe by long-distance skiers with one ski in the tracks and the other pushing off to the side, much like a speedskater pushing off. Eventually, the technique evolved to the point where both skis were out of the tracks; today, skating—which has been documented to be faster than diagonal stride—is performed on a trackless course (except for tracks installed to help skiers through some tricky turns).

In the mid-80s, skating was approved as the World Cup divided into "classical" technique (i.e., diagonal stride) and "free style" (use whatever style you prefer) races; in the Olympics and World Championships, the 50-50 split in racing goes down to two legs of classical style and two legs of skating in the relays!

"Depending on conditions, so much can happen in classical races," said Nina Kemppel, two-time Olympian. "If you or your coach 'miss the wax,' you're cooked. That kick wax can be too slippery, or it can ice-up and collect snow all along the course and it seems like you're running in high heels."

Cross country racing is a rugged mix of speed and endurance. Races are held at a variety of distances; on the World Cup tour, races range from 5- to 30-km for women, 10- to 50-km for men but there are non-World Cup 100-km races...and exhibition "sprints" of one kilometer.

While the alpine World Cup tour recognizes champions in each event as well as an overall champion, cross country skips the idea of classical and freestyle points to recognize only overall men's and women's champions.

Bread.

and Breakfast

Banana Pineapple Bread

1¹/2 cups all-purpose flour

³/4 cup whole wheat flour

¹/4 cup packed dark brown sugar

2 tablespoons wheat germ

1 tablespoon baking powder

¹/2 teaspoon baking soda

¹/4 teaspoon cinnamon

³/4 cup mashed ripe banana

1 (8-ounce) can crushed pineapple, drained

2 tablespoons canola or corn oil

1 egg white

* Combine the all-purpose flour, whole wheat flour, brown sugar, wheat germ, baking powder, baking soda and cinnamon in a large bowl.
* Mix the banana, pineapple, oil and egg white in a small bowl. Add to the dry ingredients, stirring just until moistened. Pour into a 5x9-inch loaf pan coated with nonstick cooking spray.
* Bake at 350 degrees for 50 to 55 minutes or until the bread tests done.
* Cool in the pan on a wire rack for 10 minutes. Remove to a wire rack to cool completely.
* May wrap the cooled loaf in a double thickness of foil and store in the freezer for up to 3 months.

Yield: 12 servings

Approx Per Serving: Cal 146; Prot 3 g; Carbo 28 g; T Fat 3 g;
17% Calories from Fat; Chol 0 mg; Fiber 2 g; Sod 124 mg

Cross country racer Tim Caldwell (Putney, VT) was the first U.S. nordic skier to compete

in four Olympics. He raced at the 1972, 1976, 1980, and 1984 Winter Games.

Banana Sunflower Bread

$^1/_4$ *cup vegetable oil*

$^1/_2$ *cup honey*

2 eggs

1$^3/_4$ cups whole wheat flour

1 teaspoon baking powder

$^1/_2$ *teaspoon baking soda*

$^1/_2$ *teaspoon salt*

1 cup mashed ripe bananas

$^1/_3$ *to* $^1/_2$ *cup sunflower seeds*

* Combine the oil, honey and eggs in a mixer bowl and beat well.
* Sift the whole wheat flour, baking powder, baking soda and salt together. Add to the egg mixture alternately with the bananas, beating well after each addition. Stir in the sunflower seeds. Pour into a greased 5x9-inch loaf pan.
* Bake at 350 degrees for 50 to 60 minutes or until the bread tests done.

Yield: 12 servings

Approx Per Serving: Cal 216; Prot 5 g; Carbo 32 g; T Fat 9 g;
35% Calories from Fat; Chol 46 mg; Fiber 3 g; Sod 157 mg

The World Nordic Ski Championships have come to the USA just once—in 1950.
The Opening Ceremonies and jumping were held in Lake Placid, New York, but the cross country and
nordic combined were staged in Rumford, Maine, because of a rare lack of snow in the Adirondacks.
Wendall "Chummy" Broomhall, a competitor and Rumford resident, convinced championships officials
to shift races to Maine and, at the eleventh hour, the Chisholm Ski Club staged the championships. They
haven't been back since, although they did get back to North America in 1995 when Thunder Bay,
Ontario, hosted the World Championships.

Brown Bread

2 teaspoons (heaping) baking soda
3 cups boiling water
3 cups cornmeal
4 cups graham flour
2 teaspoons (heaping) salt
2 cups molasses

* Dissolve the baking soda in the water.
* Combine the cornmeal, flour, salt and molasses in a bowl and mix well. Stir in the baking soda.
* Fill 2 greased 3-pound shortening cans $^2/_3$ full; cover with heavy foil. Place in a steamer.
* Steam for 3 hours. Remove to a wire rack to cool.

Yield: 24 servings

Approx Per Serving: Cal 187; Prot 4 g; Carbo 42 g; T Fat 1 g;
3% Calories from Fat; Chol 0 mg; Fiber 4 g; Sod 251 mg

Dartmouth ski coach Al Merrill (Lebanon, NH) was chief of course for cross country races
at the 1960 Winter Games in Squaw Valley, California, and woodsman "Chummy" Broomhall
(Rumford, ME) was chief of race. When the Olympics returned to the USA in 1980 at Lake Placid,
they flip-flopped jobs: Broomhall was chief of course and Merrill took over as chief of race.
"We were going to be working side by side, anyway," Merrill explained, "so titles didn't mean
anything, so we just decided to change 'em."

Cinnamon and Raisin Monkey Bread

3 (1-pound) loaves frozen bread dough
1/2 to 3/4 cup melted margarine
1/2 cup (about) cinnamon-sugar
1/2 cup (or more) raisins

* Let the bread dough thaw but not rise.
* Divide the dough into 1-inch portions. Shape each portion into a ball. Roll in the margarine. Coat with the cinnamon-sugar.
* Place the dough in a greased bundt pan. Sprinkle with the raisins. Let rise until the dough nearly fills the pan.
* Bake at 350 degrees for 30 minutes or until brown.
* Invert onto a serving plate.

Yield: 15 servings

Approx Per Serving: Cal 364; Prot 8 g; Carbo 55 g; T Fat 13 g;
32% Calories from Fat; Chol 0 mg; Fiber 3 g; Sod 553 mg

The only Olympic cross country medal won by an American was the 30 kilometer silver medal

earned February 5, 1976, by Bill Koch (Guilford, VT) in the first race of Olympic Winter Games XII

in Innsbruck, Austria. He wore bib No. 7, and Koch—born June 7, 1975—noted later

"Seven's always been my lucky number."

Blueberry Streusel Muffins

1/4 cup butter, softened

1/3 cup sugar

1 egg

2 1/3 cups flour

1 tablespoon baking powder

1/2 teaspoon salt

1 cup milk

1 teaspoon vanilla extract

1 1/2 cups blueberries

1/2 cup sugar

1/3 cup flour

1/2 teaspoon ground cinnamon

1/4 cup butter

* Cream 1/4 cup butter in a mixer bowl. Add 1/3 cup sugar gradually, beating at medium speed until light and fluffy.
* Add the egg and beat well.
* Mix 2 1/3 cups flour, baking powder and salt together. Add to the creamed mixture alternately with the milk, stirring well after each addition.
* Stir in the vanilla. Fold in the blueberries.
* Spoon the batter into greased muffin cups, filling 2/3 full.
* Combine 1/2 cup sugar, 1/3 cup flour and cinnamon in a bowl. Cut in 1/4 cup butter until the mixture resembles crumbs. Sprinkle over the muffin batter.
* Bake at 375 degrees for 25 to 30 minutes or until golden brown.

Yield: 18 servings

Approx Per Serving: Cal 168; Prot 3 g; Carbo 26 g; T Fat 6 g;
32% Calories from Fat; Chol 27 mg; Fiber 1 g; Sod 177 mg

John Caldwell (Putney, VT) competed in the 1952 Olympics (cross country and nordic

combined) and was head coach of the 1972 Olympic cross country team.

Oatmeal and Apple Raisin Muffins

1 cup flour

1 tablespoon baking powder

2 teaspoons cinnamon

1 teaspoon salt

1 teaspoon nutmeg

1 egg, beaten

³/4 cup milk

¹/2 cup vegetable oil

¹/3 cup sugar

1 cup raisins

1 cup chopped apple

1 cup quick-cooking oats

* Sift the flour, baking powder, cinnamon, salt and nutmeg together.
* Combine the egg, milk, oil and sugar in a bowl and stir just until blended. Add the flour mixture. Add the raisins, apple and oats, stirring just until moistened. Spoon into greased muffin cups.
* Bake at 400 degrees for 15 minutes or at 375 degrees for 20 minutes.

Yield: 15 servings

Approx Per Serving: Cal 184; Prot 3 g; Carbo 25 g; T Fat 9 g;
41% Calories from Fat; Chol 16 mg; Fiber 2 g; Sod 220 mg

Former Olympic medal winner Bill Koch (Underwood, WA) came out of retirement and
earned a place on the 1992 Olympic ski team. It was to be his fourth Olympics, and Koch was
voted by his fellow athletes to be the American flag-bearer in Opening Ceremonies.

Relay Rice Muffins

2¹/₄ cups flour

5 teaspoons baking powder

1 teaspoon salt

³/₄ cup cooked rice

1 cup milk

¹/₄ cup sugar

2 eggs, beaten

2 tablespoons melted margarine

* Mix the flour, baking powder and salt together.
* Combine the rice, milk, sugar, eggs and margarine in a bowl and mix well.
* Add the flour mixture, stirring just until moistened.
* Fill nonstick muffin cups ³/₄ full.
* Bake at 425 degrees for 30 minutes.

Yield: 12 servings

*Approx Per Serving: Cal 162; Prot 5 g; Carbo 27 g; T Fat 4 g;
21% Calories from Fat; Chol 38 mg; Fiber 1 g; Sod 358 mg*

Bill Koch set a world record in 1981 when he became the first man to skate

50 kilometers in under two hours. He raced around a 5-kilometer loop on South Pond in

Marlboro, Vermont, in 1:59.47.49; he also set a record for 30 kilometers (1:11.45).

❄ Mom's All-Purpose Coffee Cake ❄

My mother made this for us while I was growing up.
Now, when I am in Europe racing, she will send me a cake.

2 cups packed brown sugar

2 cups flour, sifted   ¹/₂ cup butter

1 cup sour cream

1 teaspoon baking soda

1 egg, beaten   1 teaspoon nutmeg

¹/₂ to 1 cup chopped pecans or walnuts, or raisins

❄ Combine the brown sugar, flour and butter in a bowl and mix until crumbly. Spread half the mixture in a greased 9x9-inch baking pan.

❄ Mix the sour cream and baking soda in a large bowl. Add the egg and nutmeg.

❄ Add the remaining crumb mixture and mix well. Spread over the crumb mixture in the pan.

❄ Sprinkle with the pecans.

❄ Bake at 350 degrees for 40 minutes; do not open the oven door.

❄ This coffee cake will have a hard caramel base and must cool slowly before being served.

❄ It's great for afternoon tea or with fruit at breakfast.

❄ May omit the pecans and sprinkle the top with cinnamon.

Yield: 6 servings

Approx Per Serving: Cal 696; Prot 8 g; Carbo 84 g; T Fat 38 g;
48% Calories from Fat; Chol 94 mg; Fiber 2 g; Sod 417 mg

Picabo Street

Picabo Street had the greatest downhill season in USA history during Winter 1995, then one-upped

herself in the 1996 season. She won three more races that year en route to her second straight

World Cup crown, earned the super G bronze medal at the World Championships and then DH gold

in Sierra Nevada, Spain, making her the first American DH world champ. Picabo skied early but turned

to racing when her school in Sun Valley added a weekly racing program. "I always wanted to race the

boys," she says. Picabo resides in Portland, Oregon.

Strawberry Coffee Cake

¹/₂ cup sugar

1 cup flour

2 teaspoons baking powder

¹/₂ teaspoon salt

¹/₂ cup milk

2 eggs

2 tablespoons melted butter

1¹/₂ cups sliced fresh strawberries

¹/₂ cup flour

¹/₂ cup sugar

¹/₄ cup butter, softened

¹/₄ cup chopped pecans

❋ Combine ¹/₂ cup sugar, 1 cup flour, baking powder, salt, milk, eggs and 2 tablespoons melted butter in a mixer bowl. Beat for 2 minutes.
❋ Spoon into a greased 8x8-inch baking pan. Top with the strawberries. Sprinkle with a mixture of ¹/₂ cup flour, ¹/₂ cup sugar, ¹/₄ cup butter and pecans.
❋ Bake at 350 degrees for 35 to 40 minutes or until the coffee cake tests done.
❋ May substitute fresh blueberries for the strawberries.

Yield: 9 servings

Approx Per Serving: Cal 286; Prot 4 g; Carbo 42 g; T Fat 12 g;
36% Calories from Fat; Chol 70 mg; Fiber 2 g; Sod 291 mg

The U.S. records for most national championships are held by Nancy Fiddler (Crowley Lake, CA),

who collected 15 between 1986 and 1993. She didn't start skiing until she was a student at

Bates College in Maine, then quit for six years before returning to cross country in the mid-1980s.

Sugar-Free Date Coffee Cake

¹/₃ cup mashed banana

¹/₂ cup butter, softened

3 eggs

1 teaspoon vanilla extract

1¹/₄ cups water

3 cups unbleached flour

1 teaspoon baking soda

2 teaspoons baking powder

1¹/₂ cups chopped dates

¹/₃ cup chopped pecans

¹/₃ cup flaked coconut

¹/₃ cup chopped dates

* Blend the banana and butter in a bowl until creamy. Add the eggs, vanilla and water and mix well.
* Stir in the flour, baking soda and baking powder. Add 1¹/₂ cups dates and mix well. Spoon into an oiled and floured 9x13-inch baking pan. Sprinkle a mixture of the pecans, coconut and remaining ¹/₃ cup dates over the batter.
* Bake at 350 degrees for 20 to 25 minutes or until the coffee cake tests done.
* Cool the coffee cake in the pan.

Yield: 10 servings

Approx Per Serving: Cal 361; Prot 7 g; Carbo 53 g; T Fat 15 g;
36% Calories from Fat; Chol 89 mg; Fiber 3 g; Sod 248 mg

The first official cross country World Cup race was held December 20, 1978, at Telemark

resort in Wisconsin, and the first race, a 5-kilometer race, was won by Alison Owen-Spencer

(Anchorage, AK). She also won a 10-kilometer non-World-Cup race the next day.

Chair-Lift Granola

6 cups rolled oats

1¹/₂ cups wheat germ

1¹/₂ cups dry milk powder

1 cup whole wheat flour

1 cup sunflower seeds

1 cup Grape-Nuts cereal

¹/₂ cup buckwheat

1 cup vegetable oil

¹/₂ cup honey

2 tablespoons molasses

1 teaspoon vanilla extract

2 cups raisins

1 cup chopped prunes

1 cup chopped dates

1 cup chopped dried apricots

* Combine the oats, wheat germ, dry milk powder, whole wheat flour, sunflower seeds, cereal and buckwheat in a large heavy roaster and mix well.
* Combine the oil, honey, molasses and vanilla in a saucepan. Heat until blended, stirring frequently. Pour over the oat mixture and mix well.
* Bake at 300 degrees for 45 to 60 minutes, stirring every 15 minutes. Remove from the oven. Let stand until cool.
* Add the raisins, prunes, dates and apricots and mix well.
* Store in airtight containers.

Yield: 30 (¹/₂-cup) servings

Approx Per Serving: Cal 337; Prot 8 g; Carbo 55 g; T Fat 12 g;
55% Calories from Fat; Chol 1 mg; Fiber 6 g; Sod 49 mg

Spiced Apple Pancakes

1 egg
1 cup buttermilk
2 tablespoons vegetable oil
1 cup flour
1 tablespoon sugar
1 teaspoon baking powder
1/2 teaspoon baking soda
1/2 teaspoon salt
1/4 teaspoon cinnamon
1/2 cup grated apple
Cider Sauce

* Beat the egg with the buttermilk and oil in a medium bowl. Add the flour, sugar, baking powder, baking soda, salt and cinnamon and mix well. Stir in the apple.
* Ladle 1/4 cup batter at a time onto a hot greased griddle. Bake until golden brown on both sides, turning once.
* Serve with Cider Sauce.

Yield: 12 (1-pancake) servings

Approx Per Serving: Cal 206; Prot 2 g; Carbo 34 g; T Fat 7 g;
30% Calories from Fat; Chol 29 mg; Fiber 1 g; Sod 218 mg

Cider Sauce

1 cup sugar
2 tablespoons cornstarch
1/2 teaspoon pumpkin pie spice
2 cups apple cider
2 tablespoons lemon juice
1/4 cup butter

* Mix the sugar, cornstarch and pumpkin pie spice in a saucepan. Stir in the cider and lemon juice gradually.
* Cook over medium heat until the mixture thickens and comes to a boil, stirring constantly. Boil for 1 minute; remove from the heat. Blend in the butter.

Three-Grain Waffles

1 cup oat bran
³/₄ cup yellow cornmeal
¹/₄ cup flour
2 tablespoons sugar
1¹/₂ teaspoons baking powder
¹/₂ teaspoon salt
2 eggs, beaten
1³/₄ to 2 cups skim milk
3 tablespoons vegetable oil
1 teaspoon vanilla extract

* Process the oat bran in a food processor until pulverized. Add the cornmeal, flour, sugar, baking powder and salt. Process just until mixed.
* Combine the eggs, 1³/₄ cups milk, oil and vanilla in a bowl and mix well. Add the oat bran mixture and mix well. Add enough of the remaining ¹/₄ cup milk to make the batter of desired consistency.
* Bake the waffles on a hot waffle iron using the manufacturer's directions.
* Serve with maple syrup and fruit or yogurt.

Yield: 6 servings

Approx Per Serving: Cal 252; Prot 10 g; Carbo 37 g; T Fat 10 g;
36% Calories from Fat; Chol 72 mg; Fiber 4 g; Sod 329 mg

Mike Gallagher (Pittsfield, VT) competed in three Winter Olympics during his
13 years on the U.S. Ski Team (1964, 1968, 1972). In 1984, he was head coach of the
U.S. Olympic squad in Sarajevo.

❄ Rømmegrøt ❄
(Sour Cream Porridge)

Every Nordic skier has to visit Norway at least once in his or her lifetime.
When pickled herring and boiled potatoes don't cut it any longer, Rømmegrøt can
pack a whole lot of calories into a little bowl.

4 cups whipping cream   ¹/₂ cup buttermilk
1 cup semolina or cream of wheat
1 quart whole milk   Salt to taste
2 to 3 tablespoons melted butter
2 to 3 tablespoons sugar   Cinnamon to taste

* Heat the whipping cream in a large saucepan. Whisk in the buttermilk. Pour into a bowl. Let stand, covered, for 8 hours or until thickened.
* Place 1 quart of the buttermilk mixture in a large saucepan. Simmer for 15 minutes.
* Stir in the semolina. Bring to a boil. Skim off the butterfat as it rises to the top.
* Bring the milk to a boil in another saucepan.
* Stir enough of the milk into the porridge to make of the desired consistency. Season with salt.
* Spoon into bowls. Top with melted butter, sugar and cinnamon.
* Serve with salted dried meat and berry juice.
* May substitute purchased sour cream for the whipping cream-buttermilk mixture; do not use low-fat sour cream.

Yield: 8 servings

Approx Per Serving: Cal 628; Prot 9 g; Carbo 32 g; T Fat 53 g;
74% Calories from Fat; Chol 192 mg; Fiber 1 g; Sod 229 mg

Luke Bodensteiner

Three-time national cross country champion Luke Bodensteiner recently joined the

U.S. Ski Team Staff to manage and promote cross country race programs.

He is a two-time Olympian and NCAA champ. Luke began skiing at 10 when his family

moved from Florida to Wisconsin. He's written a book, Endless Winter. *He and his*

wife, Vibeke, live in Heber City, Utah.

Disabled Skiing

Skiing for the physically disabled can trace its roots to post-World War II Europe. Immediately after the war, Austria, Germany, and Switzerland began running ski programs for amputees as part of the rehabilitation process. These programs made their way into the U.S. in the 1950s, but it wasn't until the late 1960s that the sport began to be organized in this country.

Disabled skiing involves persons with mobility impairments, including amputees, paraplegics, post-polio, or prenatal German measles, plus persons with visual impairments—even total blindness.

Skiing for the disabled began as a recreational sport, but it wasn't long before competition programs developed. The learn-to-ski and competition programs conducted by these groups actively assist the USDST by hosting entry-level and advanced competitions, thus providing feeder programs for potential athletes in the USDST system.

The U.S. Disabled Ski Team has two divisions: alpine and cross country. Both teams compete internationally. Each team takes part in a variety of domestic and international competitions, including World Championships and Paralympics. Disabled skiing was an exhibition sport in the 1984 and 1988 Winter Olympics.

In most disabled competitions, skiers are classified according to types of disability. Physically impaired skiers compete in "LW" categories. There can be as many as 12 categories depending on the status of the disability. Blind or partially sighted skiers compete in "B" categories.

A continuing goal of the USDST is the integration, where applicable and feasible, of its members into able-bodied competitions. USDST alpine athletes compete each year in the U.S. Alpine Championships for able-bodied skiers and have their own disabled championships, too, while the Cross Country Disabled Championships are integrated into the U.S. Cross Country Championships each year.

The alpine national disabled champions (and various individual races) have gone to an adjusted-time handicap formula that attempts to fairly lump all disabled skiers in one overall final-time set of results, according to a specific handicap formula (disability, junior/senior). This replaces the previous system, which broke out everyone by disability class.

Salads and Sandwiches

Chicken, Brown Rice and Herb Soup

2 pounds chicken pieces

4 quarts water

2¹/₂ medium onions, sliced

1 cup sliced celery

3 large carrots, sliced

1¹/₂ teaspoons chopped fresh parsley

¹/₂ teaspoon rosemary

¹/₂ teaspoon thyme

¹/₂ teaspoon savory

¹/₂ cup barley

¹/₂ cup brown rice

Salt and pepper to taste

1 (16-ounce) can crushed tomatoes

2 cups tomato juice

* Rinse the chicken. Combine the chicken, water, onions, celery, carrots, parsley, rosemary, thyme and savory in a stockpot.
* Simmer for 2 hours, stirring occasionally. Remove the chicken to a platter.
* Chop the chicken, discarding the skin and bones. Return the chicken to the stockpot. Add the barley and brown rice and mix well. Season with salt and pepper.
* Simmer for 1 hour or until the rice and barley are tender, stirring occasionally. Stir in the undrained tomatoes and tomato juice.
* Cook just until heated through.
* Ladle into soup bowls.

Yield: 12 servings

Approx Per Serving: Cal 164; Prot 14 g; Carbo 20 g; T Fat 3 g;
18% Calories from Fat; Chol 34 mg; Fiber 4 g; Sod 259 mg

Championship Gazpacho

3 to 6 large cloves of garlic, crushed

2 pounds ripe tomatoes, peeled, seeded

2 green bell peppers, cut into quarters

1 onion, cut into quarters

2 cucumbers, cut into chunks

2 to 4 slices dry white bread

¹/₄ cup olive oil

¹/₂ cup red wine vinegar

¹/₂ to 1 cup water

1 teaspoon coarse salt

* Process each vegetable separately in a food processor to a medium-coarse texture.
* Process the bread in a food processor to make fine crumbs.
* Combine the garlic, tomatoes, green peppers, onion, cucumbers, bread crumbs, oil, vinegar, water and salt in a bowl and mix well. Chill well.
* This is not a watery soup.
* Serve with cold fino sherry and European-style olives.

Yield: 4 servings

Approx Per Serving: Cal 296; Prot 6 g; Carbo 37 g; T Fat 16 g;
49% Calories from Fat; Chol 1 mg; Fiber 6 g; Sod 702 mg

The first gold medal in nordic skiing at the international level for an American

disabled skier went to Dartmouth student Rob Walsh (Hanover, NH), in the Paralympics,

as they were called then, in 1988 in Innsbruck, Austria.

Hearty Lentil Soup

5 ounces dried lentils

1 cup chopped carrots

$^1/_2$ cup chopped celery

$^1/_2$ cup chopped onion

2 tablespoons margarine

1 teaspoon thyme

1 bay leaf

1 clove of garlic, minced

$^1/_8$ teaspoon salt

3 vegetable bouillon cubes

$1^1/_2$ quarts water

* Sort and rinse the lentils.
* Sauté the carrots, celery and onion in the margarine in a stockpot. Add the lentils, thyme, bay leaf, garlic and salt and mix well.
* Cook for 1 minute, stirring constantly.
* Add the bouillon cubes and water and mix well. Bring to a boil; reduce the heat.
* Simmer, covered, until the lentils are tender, stirring occasionally. Discard the bay leaf.
* Ladle into soup bowls.

Yield: 6 servings

Approx Per Serving: Cal 131; Prot 7 g; Carbo 17 g; T Fat 4 g;
28% Calories from Fat; Chol <1 mg; Fiber 4 g; Sod 681 mg

Tofu Chili

1 (15-ounce) can tomato sauce
1¹/2 cups cooked black beans
2 cups chopped red or green bell peppers
1 onion, chopped
3 cloves of garlic, finely chopped
¹/2 cup (or more) chopped fresh cilantro
2 teaspoons cumin
3 tablespoons chili powder
2 teaspoons baking cocoa
Cinnamon and ground cloves to taste
Chopped fresh or canned hot peppers to taste
1 pound frozen extra-firm tofu, thawed, drained, torn into bite-size pieces
³/4 cup shredded Monterey Jack cheese

* Combine the tomato sauce, beans, bell peppers, onion, garlic, cilantro, cumin, chili powder, baking cocoa, cinnamon, cloves and hot peppers in a stockpot and mix well.
* Cook until the vegetables are tender, stirring occasionally. Stir in the tofu. Remove from the heat.
* Ladle into soup bowls. Sprinkle with the cheese.
* Serve with tortilla chips.
* May substitute 1 pound drained cooked ground beef, turkey or chicken for tofu. May substitute shredded Cheddar cheese for shredded Monterey Jack cheese. May substitute pinto beans for black beans.

Yield: 4 servings

Approx Per Serving: Cal 330; Prot 23 g; Carbo 35 g; T Fat 14 g;
34% Calories from Fat; Chol 19 mg; Fiber 11 g; Sod 825 mg

Old-Fashioned Turkey and Dressing Soup

10 to 12 cups water

6 chicken bouillon cubes

2 onions, chopped

4 potatoes, peeled, cubed

2 cups sliced carrots

1 turnip, peeled, cubed

6 ribs celery, sliced

1/4 head cabbage, sliced

1/4 teaspoon pepper

Salt to taste

1 bay leaf

1 tablespoon chopped parsley

3 cups chopped cooked turkey

4 cups corn bread dressing

* Bring the water to a boil in a large kettle. Add the chicken bouillon cubes, stirring until dissolved.
* Add the onions, potatoes, carrots, turnip, celery, cabbage, pepper, salt to taste, bay leaf and parsley.
* Simmer until the vegetables are tender, stirring occasionally. Add the turkey and corn bread dressing.
* Simmer until heated through.
* Remove the bay leaf before serving.

Yield: 12 servings

Approx Per Serving: Cal 198; Prot 14 g; Carbo 29 g; T Fat 3 g;
12% Calories from Fat; Chol 27 mg; Fiber 3 g; Sod 960 mg

Hot-and-Sour Vegetable Soup

1 medium onion, cut into halves, slivered

3 carrots, sliced thin diagonally

2 tablespoons vegetable oil

3 cloves of garlic, minced

1 tablespoon minced fresh ginger

4 cups defatted chicken broth

1 cup water

2 tablespoons soy sauce

2 cups thinly sliced mushrooms

1 bunch watercress, stemmed

8 ounces snow peas

1 cup fresh bean sprouts

1/4 cup rice wine vinegar

Sesame oil and chili oil to taste

* Sauté the onion and carrots in the oil in a heavy saucepan over medium heat for 3 minutes. Add the garlic and ginger.
* Cook for 1 minute, stirring constantly. Stir in the chicken broth, water and soy sauce.
* Bring to a boil; reduce the heat. Simmer, partially covered, for 2 minutes.
* Add the mushrooms and watercress. Simmer, partially covered, for 1 minute; remove from the heat.
* Stir in the snow peas and bean sprouts. Let stand, covered, for 2 minutes.
* Stir in the vinegar, sesame oil and chili oil. Cook for 1 minute or until heated through.
* Adjust the seasonings.

Yield: 8 servings

Approx Per Serving: Cal 85; Prot 5 g; Carbo 10 g; T Fat 4 g;
37% Calories from Fat; Chol 0 mg; Fiber 3 g; Sod 439 mg

Blueberry Hill Tossed Salad

1 clove of garlic

1 medium head romaine lettuce, torn into bite-size pieces

*2 heads iceberg lettuce, Boston lettuce, escarole or equal amount of
spinach, torn into bite-size pieces*

2 medium tomatoes, chopped

1 small cucumber, finely chopped

1 small white or red onion, sliced into thin rings

Sections of 1 navel orange

$^1/_2$ cup seedless grapes   4 or 5 radishes, sliced

$^1/_2$ avocado, finely chopped

2 tablespoons crumbled Roquefort cheese

1 (2-ounce) can rolled anchovies

Olive Oil and Wine Vinegar Dressing

* Rub a salad bowl with the garlic. Place the romaine lettuce and iceberg lettuce in the bowl. Cover with waxed paper.
* Layer the tomatoes, cucumber, onion, orange sections, grapes, radishes, avocado, cheese and undrained anchovies on waxed paper. Chill, covered with plastic wrap, until serving time. Remove the plastic wrap and waxed paper. Add to the salad bowl and toss to mix.
* Add the Olive Oil and Wine Vinegar Dressing to the salad, tossing to mix.

Yield: 8 servings

*Approx Per Serving: Cal 136; Prot 4 g; Carbo 11 g; T Fat 10 g;
60% Calories from Fat; Chol 5 mg; Fiber 4 g; Sod 35 mg*

Olive Oil and Wine Vinegar Dressing

$^1/_4$ cup olive oil   Salt and pepper to taste

1 clove of garlic, minced

1 teaspoon Worcestershire sauce

$1^1/_2$ tablespoons wine vinegar

* Combine the olive oil, salt, pepper, garlic, Worcestershire sauce and wine vinegar in a covered container. Shake well.

Go-with-Everything Salad

1 cup sugar

3/4 cup vinegar

1/2 cup vegetable oil

1 teaspoon celery seeds

Salt and pepper to taste

1 (16-ounce) can French-style green beans, drained

1 (16-ounce) can white corn, drained

3/4 cup chopped green onions

1 (16-ounce) can tiny green peas, drained

1 (4-ounce) jar pimentos, drained

1 (4-ounce) jar sliced mushrooms, drained

1 cup chopped celery

3/4 cup chopped green bell pepper

* Combine the sugar, vinegar, oil, celery seeds, salt and pepper in a saucepan.
* Cook over low heat until the sugar and salt are dissolved, stirring frequently. Let stand until cool.
* Combine the green beans, corn, green onions, green peas, pimentos, mushrooms, celery and green pepper in a salad bowl and toss well.
* Pour the cooled dressing over the vegetables and toss well. Chill for 8 hours to overnight before serving.

Yield: 12 servings

Approx Per Serving: Cal 213; Prot 3 g; Carbo 32 g; T Fat 10 g;
42% Calories from Fat; Chol 0 mg; Fiber 4 g; Sod 323 mg

Jeff Pagels (Green Bay, WI), the first sit-skier on the U.S. cross country disabled team,

was 36 when he was paralyzed below the waist after a tree fell on him. He went on

to win two gold medals in cross country skiing at the 1992 Paralympics in Tignes, France,

winning the 5-kilometer and 10-kilometer races.

All-Star Lentil Salad

1 pound dried lentils

5 cups water

1 teaspoon salt

³/4 cup olive oil

¹/4 cup red wine vinegar

³/4 cup chopped onion

1 clove of garlic, minced

1 teaspoon freshly ground pepper

¹/2 teaspoon Worcestershire sauce

* Sort and rinse the lentils.
* Combine the lentils, water and salt in a saucepan.
* Simmer for 35 minutes, stirring occasionally; drain. Stir in the olive oil. Cool to room temperature.
* Mix the vinegar, onion, garlic, pepper and Worcestershire sauce in a salad bowl. Add the lentils and toss to mix.
* Garnish with chopped tomato and chopped parsley.

Yield: 6 servings

Approx Per Serving: Cal 503; Prot 22 g; Carbo 46 g; T Fat 28 g;
48% Calories from Fat; Chol 0 mg; Fiber 9 g; Sod 367 mg

Spinach Salad with Honey-Mustard Dressing

6 tablespoons vegetable oil

2 tablespoons cider vinegar

2 tablespoons honey

2 tablespoons Dijon mustard

2 tablespoons toasted sesame seeds

1 clove of garlic, minced

1/2 teaspoon freshly ground pepper

2 bunches spinach

Tops of 4 green onions, chopped

1 large orange, peeled, cut into half-slices

4 slices bacon, crisp-fried, crumbled

* Combine the oil, vinegar, honey, mustard, sesame seeds, garlic and pepper in a jar with an airtight lid and shake to mix well. Chill until serving time.
* Combine the spinach, green onions and orange in a large bowl and mix well. Add the dressing, tossing to mix well.
* Spoon onto serving plates. Top with bacon.
* Serve immediately.

Yield: 4 servings

Approx Per Serving: Cal 332; Prot 7 g; Carbo 20 g; T Fat 27 g;
69% Calories from Fat; Chol 5 mg; Fiber 5 g; Sod 290 mg

Fruit Salad with Poppy Seed Dressing

1 (11-ounce) can mandarin oranges, drained

1 apple, chopped

1 banana, sliced

1 avocado, chopped

1 (20-ounce) can pineapple chunks, drained

1/4 cup raisins

1/4 cup chopped pecans

1/4 cup orange juice

1/4 cup vegetable oil

1/3 cup (or less) honey

1/2 teaspoon lemon juice

1/2 tablespoon poppy seeds

1/4 teaspoon salt

1/4 teaspoon prepared mustard

* Combine the mandarin oranges, apple, banana, avocado, pineapple, raisins and pecans in a bowl and mix well.
* Mix the orange juice, oil, honey, lemon juice, poppy seeds, salt and mustard in a jar. Shake, covered, until blended. Pour over the fruit salad and toss gently.
* Chill for 2 hours before serving.

Yield: 8 servings

Approx Per Serving: Cal 289; Prot 2 g; Carbo 45 g; T Fat 13 g;
39% Calories from Fat; Chol 0 mg; Fiber 5 g; Sod 76 mg

Orange and Onion Salad

3 oranges, peeled, sliced

1 cup seedless green grape halves

1 small red onion, thinly sliced

¹/₂ cup chopped pecans

¹/₂ cup olive oil

3 tablespoons lemon juice

1 tablespoon honey

1 teaspoon prepared mustard

¹/₄ teaspoon salt

Pepper to taste

6 cups torn salad greens, chilled

* Combine the oranges, grapes, red onion and pecans in a salad bowl and mix well.
* Combine the olive oil, lemon juice, honey, prepared mustard, salt and pepper in a bowl, stirring with a fork until blended. Pour over the orange mixture, tossing to coat.
* Chill, covered, for 4 to 6 hours. Toss with the chilled salad greens in a salad bowl just before serving.
* May substitute one 11-ounce can mandarin oranges for orange slices.

Yield: 6 servings

Approx Per Serving: Cal 319; Prot 3 g; Carbo 25 g; T Fat 25 g;
68% Calories from Fat; Chol 0 mg; Fiber 4 g; Sod 106 mg

Peanut Butter and Banana Sandwiches

5 teaspoons butter, softened

10 slices bread

¹/₂ cup creamy peanut butter

2 ripe bananas, mashed

2 tablespoons butter

* Spread 5 teaspoons butter on the bread slices.
* Spread a mixture of the peanut butter and bananas on 5 of the bread slices. Top with the remaining bread slices.
* Toast the sandwiches in 2 tablespoons butter in a skillet until light brown on both sides, turning once.

Yield: 5 servings

Approx Per Serving: Cal 419; Prot 12 g; Carbo 45 g; T Fat 23 g;
48% Calories from Fat; Chol 25 mg; Fiber 3 g; Sod 494 mg

Diana Golden (Lincoln, MA) led a 1-2-3 sweep of medals at the 1988 Olympic Winter Games,

where disabled skiing was an exhibition event with a giant slalom. Cathy Gentil (Torrance, CA) took the

silver medal, with Martha Hill (Winter Park, CO)–like Golden, a Dartmouth graduate–earning bronze.

Pecan Raisin Sandwich Spread

1 egg

1 cup sugar

Grated peel and juice of 2 lemons

¹/₂ cup margarine

1 cup mayonnaise

1 cup finely chopped raisins

1 cup finely chopped pecans

* Beat the egg in a mixer bowl until pale yellow.
* Combine the egg, sugar, lemon peel and lemon juice in a saucepan and mix well.
* Cook over low heat until thickened, stirring constantly. Stir in the margarine and mayonnaise.
* Add the raisins and pecans and mix well.
* Store in the refrigerator or freezer.

Yield: 16 servings

Approx Per Serving: Cal 316; Prot 2 g; Carbo 31 g; T Fat 22 g;
60% Calories from Fat; Chol 21 mg; Fiber 2 g; Sod 152 mg

Sarah Billmeier (Yarmouth, ME), who lost her left leg above the knee when she was five years old, was just
14 when she competed in her first major international ski race—at the 1992 Paralympics in Tignes,
France. She came home from the so-called Disabled Olympics with three gold medals. She won downhill
and giant slalom and tied for the gold medal in super G.

Freestyle Skiing

Freestyle skiing is a three-event sport, mixing the graceful twists and twirls of acro-skiing with the pulsating speed and excitement of racing through the snowy bumps in moguls, and then perhaps the biggest adrenaline "rush," aerials.

The sport's name comes from the early days when skiers tried to establish a free style as opposed to the more traditional racing side of alpine. They purposely chose the name to show they were free to use whatever style they wanted on skis.

In the early days, freestyle consisted of one run that included all the elements: a skier had to demonstrate ballet-like spins and twirls, had to ski through some moguls, and had to throw in an aerial maneuver at some point. Eventually, the three distinct elements were broken into separate events; a skier who competes in all three events is known as a "combined" skier and major competitions, from the Olympics to Nor Ams and the Chevy Truck U.S. Freestyle Championships, include a combined calculation based on how someone skied in acro, aerials, and moguls.

Aerials is the "grabber," the calling card for the sport. A skier is launched from a specially designed jump, or "kicker," and can go 50 or more feet above the snowy landing hill. In the air, they perform twists and flips before trying to land upright; skiers may not attempt inverted aerials (i.e., their feet go above their head) until they've been certified by their coaches after hours of performing the maneuver(s) into a splash pool in summer.

In moguls, skiers are judged on how well they ski a line (route) down the course and how well they perform "air," i.e., maneuvers off two midcourse jumps. A panel of judges awards specific scores for technique and a skier's two airs. There also is a factor based on how quickly the run is skied.

Acro skiing is the more subtle contrast to the electrifying and slam-bang of aerials and moguls. Highly athletic in its own way, acro (formerly known as ballet) has been likened to the beauty and skill of figure skating on skis.

"I think it's cooler looking than figure skating," said Trace Worthington, 1995 World Championships gold medalist and World Cup aerials champion. "What the acro skiers do takes incredible talent."

Entrées

Stir-Fry Chicken

1 pound boned chicken

1 tablespoon vegetable oil

1 (16-ounce) package frozen green peas

1 (16-ounce) package frozen stir-fry vegetables

1 (16-ounce) package frozen oriental vegetables

1 teaspoon sugar   2 tablespoons lemon juice

¹/₄ cup Worcestershire sauce

1 clove of garlic, minced   1 tablespoon cornstarch

1 (5-ounce) package seasoned yellow rice, cooked

1 (5-ounce) package seasoned Spanish rice, cooked

* Rinse the chicken and pat dry; cut into strips.
* Heat the oil to 300 degrees in an electric skillet. Add the chicken.
* Stir-fry until the chicken is no longer pink. Add the frozen vegetables and mix well.
* Stir-fry for 10 minutes. Stir in a mixture of the sugar, lemon juice, Worcestershire sauce, garlic and cornstarch.
* Cook for 5 minutes, stirring constantly. Stir in the rice.
* May substitute turkey or beef for chicken. May serve over rice instead of including rice in the mixture.

Yield: 12 servings

Approx Per Serving: Cal 210; Prot 7 g; Carbo 34 g; T Fat 3 g;
13% Calories from Fat; Chol 17 mg; Fiber 3 g; Sod 547 mg

Former world champion Lane Spina (Reno, NV) is the only athlete to have won a medal at
each of the first four World Freestyle Ski Championships. In 1986, he earned the silver
medal in what was then known as ballet at the first official World Freestyle Championships in
Tignes, France; in 1989, Spina was silver medalist in Oberjoch, then-still-West Germany;
in 1991, he was gold medal winner at Lake Placid, New York; and in 1993, he took the
bronze at Altenmarkt, Austria.

Raspberry and Peach Chicken

¹/2 cup fresh or frozen unsweetened raspberries

1 small peach, peeled, sliced

2¹/2 tablespoons peach brandy

2 tablespoons honey

4 (4-ounce) boneless skinless chicken breast halves

¹/4 cup flour

¹/4 teaspoon salt

¹/4 teaspoon pepper

1 tablespoon vegetable oil

* Combine the raspberries, peach, peach brandy and honey in a blender or food processor container. Process on High for 1 minute. Pour into a saucepan.
* Cook just until heated through, stirring frequently. Reduce the heat and keep warm.
* Rinse the chicken and pat dry. Coat with a mixture of the flour, salt and pepper.
* Cook the chicken in the oil in a 10-inch skillet over medium heat for 12 to 14 minutes or until the chicken is cooked through, turning once.
* Spoon some of the raspberry sauce on each serving plate. Top with chicken. Drizzle with the remaining raspberry sauce.
* Garnish with additional raspberries and peach slices.
* May substitute apple juice for peach brandy.

Yield: 4 servings

Approx Per Serving: Cal 265; Prot 28 g; Carbo 18 g; T Fat 7 g;
23% Calories from Fat; Chol 72 mg; Fiber 1 g; Sod 197 mg

Trace (The Ace) Worthington (Park City, UT) became the first skier from any nation to win two gold medals at the same World Freestyle Championships when he earned the aerials and combined titles at the 1995 World Championships in La Clusaz, France. Coincidentally, Worthington's first World Cup win came at La Clusaz in 1990–and he won both aerials and combined that weekend.

Quick Chicken Pockets

3 cups chopped chicken breast

2 tablespoons vegetable oil

1 envelope Italian spaghetti seasoning mix

²/₃ cup water

2 tablespoons tomato paste

1 cup chopped green bell pepper

3 pita bread rounds

1 cup shredded mozzarella cheese or grated Parmesan cheese

* Rinse the chicken and pat dry.
* Brown the chicken in the oil in a skillet over medium heat.
* Add a mixture of the spaghetti seasoning, water and tomato paste and mix well. Stir in the green pepper.
* Bring to a boil; reduce the heat. Simmer for 1 to 3 minutes or until thickened, stirring occasionally.
* Cut each pita round in half. Fill each half with the chicken mixture.
* Top with the cheese before serving.

Yield: 6 servings

Approx Per Serving: Cal 319; Prot 29 g; Carbo 24 g; T Fat 12 g;
33% Calories from Fat; Chol 74 mg; Fiber 1 g; Sod 919 mg

Jan Bucher Carmichael (Salt Lake City) was a figure skater when she was young.

She broke an ankle and switched to skiing, then went on to win the world ballet championship

twice, eight World Cup ballet titles, 64 individual World Cup events, and three U.S. titles.

Ground Turkey and Zucchini Casserole

1 pound ground turkey

1¹/₄ cups chopped onion

1 tablespoon vegetable oil

1 teaspoon salt

1 teaspoon basil

1 teaspoon minced garlic

5 cups cooked sliced zucchini

3 ounces shredded Swiss cheese

1 (10-ounce) can cream of mushroom soup

1 cup sour cream

4 slices bread, crumbled

* Brown the turkey and onion in the oil in a skillet, stirring frequently. Stir in the salt, basil and garlic.
* Spread in a greased 9x13-inch baking dish. Layer half the zucchini, cheese and remaining zucchini over the ground turkey mixture.
* Combine the soup and sour cream in a small bowl and mix well. Spoon over the casserole. Top with the bread crumbs.
* Bake at 350 degrees for 30 minutes.

Yield: 4 servings

Approx Per Serving: Cal 627; Prot 36 g; Carbo 35 g; T Fat 39 g;
55% Calories from Fat; Chol 117 mg; Fiber 6 g; Sod 1443 mg

Aerialist Eric Bergoust (Missoula, MT) set a points record on the night

of February 3, 1996, when his twists, somersaults, and landings received

247.51 points from the judges in Kirchberg, Austria.

Gold Medal Lamb Bundles

2 pounds lamb shoulder

2 green bell peppers

2 tomatoes

1 onion

1 eggplant, peeled

1 large potato, peeled

Salt and pepper to taste

* Cut the lamb into 4 pieces. Cut the green peppers and tomatoes into halves. Cut the onion, eggplant and potato into quarters.
* Divide the lamb and vegetables among 4 sheets of baking parchment. Sprinkle with salt and pepper.
* Wrap the bundles tightly and place in a baking pan.
* Bake at 375 degrees for 3^1/$_2$ hours.
* Serve with cooking juices in the parchment.
* May substitute foil for baking parchment.
* For best results, don't add water, don't cover, don't turn the bundles and don't try to hurry the cooking.

Yield: 4 servings

Approx Per Serving: Cal 337; Prot 39 g; Carbo 19 g; T Fat 11 g;
31% Calories from Fat; Chol 118 mg; Fiber 4 g; Sod 101 mg

One-Pot Pork Chop Supper

4 (4-ounce) pork chops

6 to 8 small whole potatoes or 3 medium potatoes, cut into quarters

4 small carrots, sliced lengthwise into halves, cut into 2-inch pieces

1 teaspoon Worcestershire sauce

¹/₂ teaspoon salt

¹/₂ teaspoon pepper

1 (10-ounce) can tomato soup

¹/₂ cup water

Oregano to taste

* Sauté the pork chops in a skillet until brown on both sides, turning once. Remove the pork chops to a platter.
* Add the potatoes, carrots, Worcestershire sauce, salt and pepper to the skillet. Arrange the pork chops over the vegetables. Pour the soup and water over the layers. Sprinkle with oregano.
* Simmer for 45 to 60 minutes or until the pork chops are cooked through, stirring twice or more.

Yield: 4 servings

Approx Per Serving: Cal 469; Prot 21 g; Carbo 46 g; T Fat 23 g;
44% Calories from Fat; Chol 72 mg; Fiber 4 g; Sod 887 mg

Captain's Fish

1 (4-ounce) orange roughy fillet
1 large onion, sliced
1 potato, sliced
1 carrot, sliced
Paprika to taste
Garlic salt to taste
Pepper to taste

* Coat a large piece of heavy-duty foil with nonstick cooking spray. Place the fish in the center of the foil.
* Top with the onion, potato and carrot. Sprinkle with paprika, garlic salt and pepper.
* Fold up the foil, sealing the top and sides. Place on a baking sheet.
* Bake at 450 degrees for 25 minutes.
* Unwrap the foil carefully, avoiding the steam.

Yield: 1 serving

Approx Per Serving: Cal 449; Prot 31 g; Carbo 70 g; T Fat 5 g;
10% Calories from Fat; Chol 57 mg; Fiber 10 g; Sod 114 mg

When the Olympics formally added freestyle skiing in 1992, Donna Weinbrecht (W. Milford, NJ)
and Nelson Carmichael (Steamboat Springs, CO) didn't waste much time getting medals
for the USA. Men's and women's moguls were held the same day (February 13); Weinbrecht, the
"Jersey Girl" with the signature blonde ponytail, won the women's gold, while Carmichael
took the men's bronze medal.

❄ Grilled Scallops Over Rice ❄

*One summer evening, I decided to cook outdoors and wanted to come up
with a cool way to cook scallops. Voila–a favorite was born.*

2 cups teriyaki sauce

$^1/_2$ cup dark corn syrup or molasses

1 teaspoon garlic powder

1 pound sea scallops   1 cup rice, cooked

* Combine the teriyaki sauce, corn syrup and garlic powder in a bowl and mix well. Add the scallops.
* Marinate in the refrigerator for 1 to 2 hours.
* Remove the scallops from the marinade, reserving the marinade.
* Sear the scallops on the grill. Cook until the scallops are tinged with brown, basting occasionally. The final basting should be 3 to 5 minutes before removing the scallops from the grill.
* Serve over the rice.
* Garnish with thin lemon slices.
* Asparagus is a nice accompaniment to this dish.

Yield: 4 servings

*Approx Per Serving: Cal 502; Prot 27 g; Carbo 94 g; T Fat 3 g;
6% Calories from Fat; Chol 29 mg; Fiber 1 g; Sod 5958 mg
Nutritional profile includes entire amount of marinade.*

Ron Shepard

*It didn't take Ron Shepard long to realize that the corporate world was not his style.
The only way he would be truly fulfilled was to pursue a job in the ski industry. Ron began first
as a rep, then as a contributing writer to industry publications. Now Ron has added
management of the Master's Program for USSA. Ron has said that he needs to work and stay
active in sports because he likes to eat so much. His favorite meal is clams (they almost
stopped him from moving to the West). He lives in Park City, Utah, with his wife, Carol,
and young terrorist son Riley.*

Mediterranean Fish with Potatoes

1 pound new potatoes, unpeeled, thinly sliced
1 tablespoon olive oil
1 large onion, cut into quarters, sliced
1 clove of garlic, minced
1 teaspoon cumin
1 tablespoon coarsely grated fresh ginger
1 large green bell pepper, coarsely chopped
2 tablespoons tomato paste
2 tablespoons balsamic vinegar
Salt substitute to taste
1 pound scrod or other white fish fillets
4 small plum tomatoes, thinly sliced
1 cup chopped fresh coriander

* Brown the potatoes on both sides in the olive oil in a large nonstick skillet. Add the onion, garlic, cumin and ginger and mix well.
* Sauté for 3 to 4 minutes or until the onion is tender-crisp. Add the green pepper.
* Cook for 3 to 4 minutes, stirring constantly. Stir in the tomato paste, vinegar and salt substitute.
* Arrange the fish over the vegetables. Top with the tomatoes.
* Cook, covered, for 10 minutes for each inch of fish thickness. Arrange the fish and vegetables on serving plates. Sprinkle with the coriander.

Yield: 3 servings

Approx Per Serving: Cal 450; Prot 37 g; Carbo 50 g; T Fat 11 g;
23% Calories from Fat; Chol 76 mg; Fiber 6 g; Sod 121 mg

❄ Cayenne Shrimp ❄

³/₄ cup butter

1 bay leaf

¹/₄ cup fresh lemon juice

1 teaspoon garlic powder

1 teaspoon cayenne

1¹/₂ teaspoons lemon pepper

¹/₂ cup water

1 pound shrimp, peeled, deveined

❊ Combine the butter, bay leaf, lemon juice, garlic powder, cayenne, lemon pepper and water in a saucepan. Heat until the butter melts, stirring occasionally.

❊ Arrange the shrimp in a single layer in a shallow glass baking dish.

❊ Pour the butter sauce over the shrimp.

❊ Bake at 350 degrees for 40 minutes.

❊ Discard the bay leaf.

❊ Serve from the baking dish. Serve with lots of French bread to dip in the butter sauce.

❊ Add a salad to the meal to cut the richness.

Yield: 4 servings

Approx Per Serving: Cal 388; Prot 17 g; Carbo 2 g; T Fat 35 g;
81% Calories from Fat; Chol 247 mg; Fiber <1 g; Sod 702 mg

Bill Marolt

Bill Marolt, who was U.S. alpine skiing director during one of the U.S. Ski Team's most successful years before taking over as University of Colorado athletic director, came back to U.S. Skiing in the summer of 1996 as President and CEO. An Aspen, Colorado, native, Bill raced for the University of Colorado and competed in the 1964 Olympics. He also won three U.S. championships. He is married and has two grown daughters; he and his wife, Connie, live in Park City, Utah.

Bean Burritos

4¹/₂ teaspoons olive oil

1 medium onion, chopped

1 large green bell pepper, chopped

1 large red bell pepper, chopped

1 jalapeño, minced

2 cloves of garlic, minced

¹/₄ teaspoon salt

1 tablespoon chili powder

¹/₂ teaspoon oregano

¹/₂ teaspoon cumin

Tabasco sauce to taste

2 (16-ounce) cans pinto beans

10 flour tortillas, warmed

1 cup shredded Monterey Jack cheese

1 avocado, chopped

1 cup sour cream

1 cup salsa

* Heat the olive oil in a large skillet over medium-high heat. Add the onion, bell peppers, jalapeño, garlic and salt.
* Stir-fry for 1 minute. Stir in the chili powder, oregano, cumin and Tabasco sauce; reduce the heat.
* Cook just until the bell peppers are tender-crisp, stirring frequently. Stir in the undrained beans.
* Cook until most of the liquid has evaporated and the mixture has thickened to the desired consistency, stirring occasionally.
* Spoon the bean mixture onto the tortillas. Top with the cheese, avocado, sour cream and salsa. Fold in the ends of the tortillas and roll to enclose the filling.
* May mash the beans if preferred.

Yield: 10 servings

Approx Per Serving: Cal 395; Prot 15 g; Carbo 49 g; T Fat 17 g;
38% Calories from Fat; Chol 21 mg; Fiber 15 g; Sod 316 mg

Chile-Stuffed Peppers

4 large red or green bell peppers
8 ounces extra-lean ground beef
1 medium onion, minced
1 (16-ounce) can kidney beans, drained
1 (15-ounce) can tomato purée
1 (14-ounce) can chopped green chiles
2 teaspoons chili powder
1/2 teaspoon cumin

* Cut the bell peppers into halves; discard the seeds and membranes. Arrange cut side up in a 9x13-inch baking dish.
* Brown the ground beef with the onion in a 10-inch nonstick skillet, stirring until the ground beef is crumbly; drain. Stir in the kidney beans, tomato purée, undrained chiles, chili powder and cumin.
* Bring to a boil; reduce the heat.
* Simmer, covered, for 10 minutes, stirring frequently.
* Spoon the ground beef mixture into the bell pepper halves.
* Bake, covered, at 350 degrees for 40 to 45 minutes or until the bell peppers are tender.

Yield: 8 servings

Approx Per Serving: Cal 156; Prot 11 g; Carbo 21 g; T Fat 4 g;
21% Calories from Fat; Chol 21 mg; Fiber 6 g; Sod 1006 mg

Spaghetti Squash Primavera

1 (3-pound) spaghetti squash

8 ounces medium zucchini

1 small red bell pepper

Florets of 8 ounces broccoli

1 shallot, minced

2 tablespoons olive oil

4 ounces snow peas

1 cup whipping cream

1/4 cup butter

3/4 cup grated Parmesan cheese

1/4 teaspoon salt

Pepper to taste

* Pierce the squash with a fork. Bring to a boil in water to cover in a large saucepan; reduce the heat. Simmer, covered, for 50 to 55 minutes. Cool slightly.
* Cut the squash into halves lengthwise; discard the seeds. Scrape carefully lengthwise with a fork to separate into strands; set aside.
* Slice the zucchini diagonally 1/4 inch wide. Cut the bell pepper into 1/4-inch strips.
* Sauté the zucchini, bell pepper, broccoli and shallot in the olive oil in a large skillet over medium heat for 3 to 5 minutes. Add the snow peas.
* Sauté for 1 minute; remove from the heat.
* Heat the cream and butter just to the boiling point in a small saucepan. Stir in the cheese, salt and pepper. Toss with the squash strands.
* Spoon onto a serving platter. Top with the sautéed vegetables.
* Serve with additional cheese.

Yield: 6 servings

Approx Per Serving: Cal 402; Prot 9 g; Carbo 26 g; T Fat 31 g;
69% Calories from Fat; Chol 83 mg; Fiber 9 g; Sod 413 mg

Zesty Tofu Vegetables

4 ounces egg noodles   1 tablespoon peanut oil

3 green onions, finely chopped

3 cloves of garlic, minced

2 teaspoons minced fresh ginger

$1/2$ rib of celery, thinly sliced

1 medium zucchini, julienned

2 medium carrots, peeled, julienned

$1/2$ green bell pepper, thinly sliced

4 ounces mushrooms, thinly sliced

1 cup low-sodium chicken broth

2 cups small broccoli florets

4 ounces snow peas   1 tablespoon cornstarch

Hot pepper sauce to taste   Soy sauce to taste

1 tablespoon tahini $3/4$ teaspoon peanut butter

1 teaspoon sesame oil $1/2$ teaspoon sugar

$1/2$ loaf tofu, cut into $3/4$-inch chunks

3 green onion tops, sliced

* Cook the noodles using package directions. Rinse in cold water; drain.
* Heat the peanut oil in a heavy 12-inch skillet over medium-high heat for 1 minute. Add the chopped green onions, garlic and ginger. Stir-fry for 30 seconds.
* Add the celery, zucchini, carrots, green pepper and mushrooms. Stir-fry for 2 minutes longer.
* Stir in $1/2$ cup of the chicken broth. Simmer, covered, for 3 minutes.
* Add the broccoli and snow peas. Simmer, covered, for 2 minutes.
* Combine the remaining $1/2$ cup broth, cornstarch, hot pepper sauce, soy sauce, tahini, peanut butter, sesame oil and sugar in a bowl and mix well. Add to the skillet.
* Cook for 4 minutes or until thickened, stirring constantly. Add the noodles and tofu and mix well.
* Simmer, covered, for 2 minutes or until heated through. Spoon onto a serving platter.
* Sprinkle with the sliced green onion tops.

Yield: 4 servings

Approx Per Serving: Cal 300; Prot 14 g; Carbo 38 g; T Fat 12 g;
36% Calories from Fat; Chol 0 mg; Fiber 6 g; Sod 62 mg

Low-Cholesterol Quiche

1 (10-ounce) package frozen mixed vegetables

3 slices bread, cubed

Egg substitute equivalent to 4 eggs

2 cups skim milk

2 tablespoons sugar

1/2 teaspoon cinnamon

Salt to taste

* Cook the mixed vegetables using the package directions; drain.
* Layer the bread cubes and vegetables in a 9-inch deep-dish pie plate sprayed with nonstick cooking spray.
* Beat the egg substitute and skim milk in a mixer bowl. Add the sugar, cinnamon and salt and mix well. Pour over the layers in the pie plate.
* Bake at 350 degrees for 45 minutes or until a knife inserted near the center comes out clean.
* May add raisins or nuts or top the baked quiche with shredded cheese.

Yield: 4 servings

Approx Per Serving: Cal 218; Prot 16 g; Carbo 32 g; T Fat 3 g;
13% Calories from Fat; Chol 3 mg; Fiber 3 g; Sod 307 mg

❄ Thai Pizza ❄

This is a favorite recipe among USSA staff and athletes.

2 chicken breasts
¹/₄ cup peanut sauce   1 Boboli pizza crust
3 to 3¹/₂ cups shredded asiago cheese
1 bunch scallions, chopped
2 carrots, chopped   1 cup bean sprouts
10 mushrooms, sliced
1 red bell pepper, chopped

- ❄ Rinse the chicken.
- ❄ Combine the chicken with boiling water to cover in a 4-quart saucepan. Boil for 15 minutes; drain. Let cool for 10 minutes. Shred the chicken when it is cool enough to handle.
- ❄ Spread the peanut sauce over the pizza crust. Top with the chicken.
- ❄ Sprinkle with ¹/₂ to 1 cup of the cheese. Add the scallions, carrots, bean sprouts, mushrooms and red pepper.
- ❄ Top with the remaining cheese. Place on a preheated pizza stone.
- ❄ Bake at 375 degrees for 15 to 20 minutes or until the cheese begins to brown.
- ❄ Serve warm.

Yield: 4 servings

Approx Per Serving: Cal 802; Prot 58 g; Carbo 57 g; T Fat 39 g;
44% Calories from Fat; Chol 141 mg; Fiber 5 g; Sod 974 mg

Trisha Skalicky

Trisha Skalicky, a Minneapolis native, headed for the Rockies as soon as she graduated from the University of Minnesota in 1992. She landed in Denver and was marketing director for a leading real estate firm before being named director of the U.S. Ski Team Foundation in late 1995. Skalicky oversees the Foundation, which raises over two million dollars annually for the U.S. Ski and Snowboard Teams through fund-raisers, direct mail, a major gifts campaign, the National Ski Areas Association Gold Pass Program, and other innovative programs. She lives in Park City, Utah.

Ski Jumping

Ski jumping, with its athletes soaring through the air and going more than the length of a football field down a snowy hillside, is one of the most spectacular winter sports. It's a tricky blend of sheer power—at takeoff—and a near-scientific application of basic flight principles. "Aerodynamic" and "flying" are common words as jumpers discuss their sport or as people watch them sail down the landing hill.

The introduction of the so-called V-Technique, with a skier pushing his skis into a V-form immediately after takeoff, has revolution-ized the sport. Skiers jump farther than ever before, and they do it from a lower start at the top of the in-run and with lower takeoff speeds.

"It's such a rush when you hit that takeoff," said U.S. national champion and 1994 Olympian Randy Weber. "You're going almost 60 miles an hour and then you're in the air. You're only 10 or 12 feet off the ground but, especially as you come over the knoll of the hill and start dropping, it can seem like you've dropped out of an airplane."

Skiers hunch over their skis as they come down the in-run, gathering speed for their takeoff. They try to stay low, but not too low, before they spring forward and up, swing the tips of their 8^1/$_2$-foot skis (about 252 centimeters) out so they can ride whatever air may be on the hill. Women compete in ski jumping, but none have made it to the World Cup level.

World Cup jumps are divided into three categories: normal hill, large hill, and flying hill. Developing skiers start on much smaller hills, perhaps even as small as a 5-meter, which could be little more than snow piled up and shaped into a jump. The normal hill originally was known as a 70-meter hill but now more often is referred to as a 90-meter hill because that's about how far a skier jumps from the takeoff to the spot midway between the two skis on landing; the large hill, originally a 90-meter, is usually known today as a 115- or 120-meter.

The flying, or ski-flying, hill is the biggest of all; there are only six in the world, including Copper Peak at Ironwood, Michigan. They range any-where from 160 meters to 185.

Pasta

Serve-a-Team Lasagna

8 ounces Italian sausage   8 ounces ground beef
$^1/_2$ cup chopped onion $^1/_2$ cup chopped celery
$^1/_2$ cup chopped carrot   1 clove of garlic, chopped
1 (16-ounce) can tomatoes, chopped
1 (6-ounce) can tomato paste
1 teaspoon sugar   2 teaspoons Italian seasoning
2 eggs, beaten   2 cups ricotta cheese
$^1/_2$ cup grated Parmesan cheese
2 tablespoons chopped parsley
8 lasagna noodles, cooked
8 ounces mozzarella cheese, shredded

* Brown the sausage and ground beef in a 10-inch skillet, stirring until ground beef is crumbly; drain.
* Add the onion, celery, carrot, garlic, tomatoes, tomato paste, sugar and Italian seasoning and mix well.
* Combine the beaten eggs, ricotta cheese, Parmesan cheese and parsley in a bowl and mix well.
* Layer half the noodles, ricotta cheese mixture, remaining noodles, meat sauce and mozzarella cheese in a baking dish.
* Bake at 350 degrees for 45 to 60 minutes or until bubbly.

Yield: 12 servings

Approx Per Serving: Cal 321; Prot 20 g; Carbo 22 g; T Fat 17 g;
48% Calories from Fat; Chol 93 mg; Fiber 1 g; Sod 383 mg

Tom Kelly, a University of Wisconsin alumnus with a 20-year background in ski promotion, came to U.S. Skiing in 1986 after being marketing director for Wisconsin's Telemark resort and the American Birkebeiner, the largest ski race in North America. As director of operations for U.S. Skiing, Tom oversees all image development for the U.S. Ski Team, corporate communications, and membership service for the 50,000 U.S. Ski Association members. He and his wife, Carole, live in Park City, Utah, and have four grown children and three growing grandchildren.

❄ Ski Ball Pasta ❄

Top U.S. Ski and Snowboard Team competitors travel around the world, living out of duffel bags and eating all kinds of imaginable (and unimaginable) cuisine. But the one standard worldwide is pasta. I stumbled upon my favorite pasta dish at a U.S. Ski Team fund-raising ball, of all places, and I've re-created it here. It's easy to make, and it adds a unique distinction as a pasta dish that can be served for a family or for an elegant evening dinner with friends.

1 tablespoon olive oil   2 cloves of garlic, finely diced

2 tablespoons finely diced yellow onion   1 (16-ounce) can tomato sauce

1 (16-ounce) can crushed tomatoes   2 carrots, finely diced

2 tablespoons oregano   2 tablespoons basil

2 teaspoons ground pepper   1 tablespoon olive oil

1 teaspoon (or more) salt   16 ounces linguini or other pasta

1 teaspoon olive oil   1 cup light cream   8 teaspoons olive oil

4 cloves of garlic, finely diced $^1/_2$ cup chopped Roma tomatoes

* Heat 1 tablespoon olive oil in a medium saucepan over medium heat. Add 2 cloves of garlic and onion. Sauté for 2 minutes or until tender.
* Add the tomato sauce, crushed tomatoes, carrots, oregano, basil and pepper. Bring to a boil. Simmer, covered, until the sauce is reduced to approximately 2 cups, stirring frequently.
* Combine enough water to cover the pasta, 1 tablespoon olive oil and salt in a large stockpot. Bring to a boil. Add the pasta. Cook until al dente; do not overcook. Drain in a colander and rinse with cold water. Stir in 1 teaspoon olive oil to prevent the pasta from sticking.
* Add the cream gradually to the tomato sauce until the sauce is slightly pink. Keep warm over low heat.
* Prepare each pasta serving individually. Heat 1 teaspoon olive oil in a lightweight medium skillet. Add $^1/_8$ of the remaining garlic. Sauté for 20 to 30 seconds. Add 1 serving of pasta, mixing vigorously for 10 seconds to lightly coat the pasta. Add 2 to 4 ounces of the tomato sauce. Mix for 5 to 10 seconds or until coated. Pour the pasta onto a serving plate. Top with a tablespoon of chopped tomato. Garnish with parsley.
* Once you're good at this, you can easily serve 6 to 8 persons in about 5 minutes.
* May add 1 chopped Roma tomato to the sauce for a thicker, more tomato-rich sauce.

Yield: 8 servings

*Approx Per Serving: Cal 421; Prot 10 g; Carbo 54 g; T Fat 19 g;
40% Calories from Fat; Chol 33 mg; Fiber 4 g; Sod 724 mg*

Tom Kelly

Chicken Fettuccini

12 ounces fettuccini

2 cups chopped chicken

1 (4-ounce) can sliced mushrooms, drained

1/2 cup sliced celery

1/2 cup butter

1/2 cup light cream

1/2 cup grated Parmesan cheese

1 teaspoon salt

3/4 teaspoon pepper

* Cook the pasta using the package directions; drain.
* Rinse the chicken and pat dry.
* Sauté the chicken, mushrooms and celery in the butter in a saucepan until the chicken is cooked through and the celery is tender.
* Stir in the cream. Cook just until heated through; do not boil.
* Combine the cream sauce, hot pasta, cheese, salt and pepper in a bowl, tossing to mix well. Serve warm.

Yield: 6 servings

Approx Per Serving: Cal 505; Prot 25 g; Carbo 45 g; T Fat 25 g;
44% Calories from Fat; Chol 97 mg; Fiber 2 g; Sod 808 mg

Gordy Wren (Steamboat Springs, CO) holds a U.S. ski record which may last forever: in 1948,
he qualified for four Olympic ski teams. He was sent to St. Moritz, Switzerland, as a member of the
alpine, cross country, jumping, and nordic combined teams. Eventually, he settled on jumping:
"I was bumping into myself running from one training site to the next," he said. Worn ragged by cross-
training, he finished fifth in the Olympic event, just 2.3 points away from the bronze medal.

Seafood Fettuccini

12 ounces fettuccini
1 envelope creamy herb soup mix
2¹/₂ cups milk
1 cup half-and-half
1 cup shredded Monterey Jack cheese
8 ounces frozen shrimp, partially thawed
8 ounces snow crab, partially thawed
1 cup frozen peas, partially thawed
¹/₄ cup chopped pimento
¹/₃ cup grated Parmesan cheese

* Cook the fettuccini using the package directions; drain.
* Blend the soup mix with milk and half-and-half in a 2-quart saucepan with a fork or wire whip. Bring just to a boil. Add the Monterey Jack cheese. Cook over low heat until the Monterey Jack cheese melts, stirring constantly.
* Add the shrimp, snow crab, peas and pimento. Simmer for 3 to 4 minutes or until the shrimp and snow crab are tender.
* Toss the sauce with the hot fettuccini and Parmesan cheese.

Yield: 6 servings

Approx Per Serving: Cal 527; Prot 35 g; Carbo 57 g; T Fat 18 g;
30% Calories from Fat; Chol 147 mg; Fiber 3 g; Sod 765 mg

In 1976 Greg Windsperger (Minneapolis, MN) finished 34th in the Olympic
70-meter jumping event. After the 1980 Olympics, Windsperger took over as head coach;
he retired after the 1988 Winter Games in Calgary.

Penne with Steamed Vegetables

1 cup broccoli florets
1 cup cauliflowerets
1 cup fresh green beans, trimmed, cut into 2-inch slices
1/2 cup sliced carrot
2 medium tomatoes, chopped
1/2 cup fresh corn kernels
1/4 cup chopped red onion
1 tablespoon olive oil
1/4 cup chopped fresh basil
Salt and freshly ground pepper to taste
8 ounces penne

* Steam the broccoli, cauliflower, green beans and carrot in a steamer for 5 minutes.
* Combine the tomatoes, corn, red onion, olive oil, basil, salt and pepper in a bowl and mix well.
* Combine the penne and salt with enough water to cover in a saucepan. Cook for 10 minutes or until al dente.
* Stir 1/4 cup of the pasta cooking liquid into the tomato mixture; drain the pasta.
* Combine the steamed vegetables, tomato mixture and pasta in a bowl and mix well.
* Serve with grated Parmesan cheese.

Yield: 4 servings

Approx Per Serving: Cal 298; Prot 10 g; Carbo 55 g; T Fat 5 g;
14% Calories from Fat; Chol 0 mg; Fiber 5 g; Sod 31 mg

Mike Holland (Norwich, VT) was the first person to ski jump more than 600 feet
when he jumped 186 meters during training at the 1985 World Ski-flying Championships
in Planica, Slovenia (then part of Yugoslavia).

Title-Winners' Spaghetti

1 pound ground beef

3¹/₂ cups cooked tomatoes

¹/₃ cup chopped onion

¹/₃ cup chopped green bell pepper

¹/₂ cup catsup

1 teaspoon salt

1 cup bite-size spaghetti pieces

✳ Brown the ground beef lightly in a large skillet over medium heat, stirring until crumbly; drain.

✳ Add the tomatoes, onion, green pepper, catsup, salt and spaghetti and mix well. Cook, covered, over high heat for 5 minutes, stirring frequently.

✳ Reduce the heat; simmer for 30 minutes or until the spaghetti is tender, stirring occasionally.

✳ Serve hot.

Yield: 6 servings

Approx Per Serving: Cal 279; Prot 20 g; Carbo 25 g; T Fat 11 g;
36% Calories from Fat; Chol 56 mg; Fiber 3 g; Sod 654 mg

Most ski jumping hills are known as either "normal hill" or "large hill," depending on
how far a skier goes from the edge of the takeoff "table" to the landing spot. On a normal hill,
skiers generally go about 90 meters, about 120 meters on a large hill. Ski flying hills allow a
jumper to routinely go 185 meters, nearly the length of two football fields!

Stir-Fry Pasta with Asparagus

1 pound fresh asparagus

1 bunch green onions

1 to 2 tablespoons olive oil

2 tablespoons soy sauce

1 clove of garlic, finely chopped

1 teaspoon grated gingerroot

$^{1}/_{2}$ teaspoon Worcestershire sauce

$^{1}/_{4}$ teaspoon crushed red pepper

8 ounces vermicelli or angel hair pasta, cooked

* Trim the asparagus and cut into $1^{1}/_{2}$- to 2-inch pieces. Cut the green onions diagonally into 2-inch strips.
* Stir-fry the asparagus and green onions in the olive oil and soy sauce in a large skillet for 4 minutes.
* Add the garlic, gingerroot, Worcestershire sauce and red pepper and mix well. Add the pasta. Stir-fry until heated through.

Yield: 6 servings

Approx Per Serving: Cal 207; Prot 7 g; Carbo 34 g; T Fat 5 g;
23% Calories from Fat; Chol 0 mg; Fiber 3 g; Sod 354 mg

The first national ski championship of any sort was held in 1904 when Conrad Thompson

(Ishpeming, MI) won what was known then as the Class A championship. The meet was

held February 22, 1904, in Ishpeming; the National Ski Association was formed the following year

and at its 1912 convention, association members voted to recognize that 1904 meet as

the first official national championship.

Springtime Pasta

8 ounces fresh asparagus, trimmed

8 ounces mushrooms, sliced

1/4 cup slivered baked ham

1 medium carrot, thinly sliced

1 medium zucchini, cubed

1/4 cup butter

3 green onions with tops, sliced

1/2 cup frozen green peas, thawed

1 teaspoon dried basil

1/2 teaspoon salt

Nutmeg and white pepper to taste

1 cup whipping cream

1 (10-ounce) package angel hair pasta, cooked

1/4 cup grated Parmesan cheese

* Slice the asparagus diagonally into 1-inch pieces, leaving the tips whole.
* Sauté the asparagus, mushrooms, ham, carrot and zucchini in the butter in a large skillet over medium heat for 3 minutes, stirring occasionally. Cook, covered, for 1 minute longer.
* Add the green onions, peas, basil, salt, nutmeg, white pepper and whipping cream and mix well. Cook over high heat until bubbly, stirring constantly.
* Drain the cooked pasta. Add to the sauce mixture, tossing to coat. Add the Parmesan cheese, tossing to coat.
* Pour into a warmed serving bowl. Garnish with parsley and additional grated Parmesan cheese.

Yield: 6 servings

Approx Per Serving: Cal 443; Prot 13 g; Carbo 44 g; T Fat 25 g;
50% Calories from Fat; Chol 81 mg; Fiber 3 g; Sod 418 mg

Vegetable Lasagna

1 (12-ounce) package lasagna noodles, cooked, drained
Vegetable Sauce   2 cups ricotta cheese
Tomato Sauce   ¹/₂ cup grated Parmesan cheese

* Layer ¹/₃ of the noodles, ¹/₂ of the Vegetable Sauce and ¹/₂ cup of the ricotta cheese in a buttered 9x13-inch baking dish. Layer with ¹/₂ of the remaining noodles, remaining Vegetable Sauce and ¹/₂ cup ricotta cheese. Spread ¹/₃ cup Tomato Sauce over the layers. Layer with the remaining noodles, remaining ricotta cheese and remaining Tomato Sauce. Sprinkle with the Parmesan cheese.
* Bake at 350 degrees for 20 to 25 minutes or until heated through.

Yield: 10 servings

Approx Per Serving: Cal 343; Prot 14 g; Carbo 37 g; T Fat 16 g;
41% Calories from Fat; Chol 29 mg; Fiber 4 g; Sod 316 mg

Vegetable Sauce

1 cup minced onion   ¹/₄ to ¹/₂ teaspoon hot pepper flakes
¹/₃ cup olive oil   1 pound fresh mushrooms, coarsely chopped
2 cloves of garlic, minced   2 cups grated carrots
1 green bell pepper, finely chopped
1 red bell pepper, finely chopped   1¹/₂ cups chopped peeled eggplant
Salt and pepper to taste

* Sauté the onion with the hot pepper flakes in the olive oil in a skillet for 5 to 6 minutes or until the onion is tender but not brown. Stir in the mushrooms.
* Cook over medium heat for 3 to 4 minutes or until the mushrooms are tender.
* Add the garlic, carrots, green pepper, red pepper, eggplant, salt and pepper and mix well. Sauté for 3 to 4 minutes or until the vegetables are tender; reduce the heat.
* Cook, covered, for 15 minutes, stirring occasionally.

Tomato Sauce

15 ounces tomato purée   1 teaspoon basil
1 teaspoon oregano   2 tablespoons dry white wine

* Bring the tomato purée, basil, oregano and white wine to a boil in a saucepan; reduce the heat.
* Simmer over medium heat for 10 minutes, stirring frequently.

❄ American Macaroni ❄

Growing up with Italian parents, we always had fresh tomato sauce and Romano cheese on our macaroni. This is a casserole my dad called "American's Macaroni."

1 pound Muenster cheese

1 yellow onion, chopped

2 green bell peppers, chopped

1 tablespoon olive oil

1 pound ground beef

1¹/₂ pounds elbow macaroni

3 (10-ounce) cans tomato soup

* Shred half the cheese; thinly slice the remaining cheese.
* Sauté the onion and green peppers in the olive oil in a skillet over low heat.
* Brown the ground beef in a large skillet, stirring until crumbly; drain.
* Cook the macaroni using the package directions; drain.
* Combine the macaroni, soup, ground beef and sautéed vegetables in a bowl and mix well. Stir in the shredded cheese.
* Pour into a casserole. Top with the sliced cheese.
* Bake at 350 degrees for 30 to 45 minutes or until the casserole is bubbly and heated through and the cheese is golden brown.

Yield: 8 servings

Approx Per Serving: Cal 748; Prot 39 g; Carbo 82 g; T Fat 29 g;
35% Calories from Fat; Chol 97 mg; Fiber 3 g; Sod 1196 mg

Janine Alfano

❄

An East Coast native, Janine Alfano graduated from Dickinson College and moved to Denver, where she spent eight years handling advertising, promotions, and marketing for The Denver Post. *She joined the U.S. Ski Team Foundation in 1996. As the Director of Special Events, Janine manages all of the U.S. Ski Team's fund-raising events across the country and is responsible for developing new fund-raising ideas. She lives in Park City, Utah.*

Rotini and Crab Meat Salad

3 ribs celery, chopped
1 cucumber, sliced into rounds
4 carrots, sliced into rounds
3 green onions, chopped
Green and black olives to taste
1 (16-ounce) bottle fat-free Italian salad dressing
Tony seasoning to taste
2 (10-ounce) packages crab meat, drained, flaked
16 ounces rotini, cooked, drained

* Combine the celery, cucumber, carrots, green onions and olives in a large bowl.
* Add the salad dressing, tossing to coat. Let stand for 15 minutes.
* Add Tony seasoning, crab meat and rotini and mix well.
* Chill, covered, until serving time.

Yield: 10 servings

Approx Per Serving: Cal 258; Prot 18 g; Carbo 42 g; T Fat 2 g;
7% Calories from Fat; Chol 57 mg; Fiber 3 g; Sod 637 mg

The first Olympic nordic medal won by an American skier was the bronze earned

by Anders Haugen in ski jumping during the inaugural Winter Games, 1924,

at Chamonix, France. He didn't receive the medal, though, until (posthumously) a century later, after

a recalculation of his points showed he finished third, not fourth.

Judges' Macaroni Salad

8 ounces uncooked macaroni

1 cup chopped onion

1 cup chopped celery

$^1/_2$ cup shredded carrot

1 cup chopped cucumber

Florets of 1 bunch broccoli

$^1/_2$ cup mayonnaise

$^1/_2$ cup vegetable oil

$^1/_4$ cup vinegar

$^1/_4$ cup sugar

1 envelope Italian salad dressing mix

* Cook the macaroni using the package directions; drain.
* Combine the macaroni, onion, celery, carrot, cucumber and broccoli in a large bowl.
* Combine the mayonnaise, oil, vinegar, sugar and salad dressing mix in a medium bowl and mix well. Add to the macaroni mixture and mix gently.
* Chill until serving time.

Yield: 6 servings

Approx Per Serving: Cal 499; Prot 7 g; Carbo 45 g; T Fat 34 g;
60% Calories from Fat; Chol 11 mg; Fiber 3 g; Sod 298 mg

The Holland brothers (Norwich, VT) hold a U.S. mark which figures to
stand for a while: for a week in 1990, all three brothers were a national champion
simultaneously–Mike as the reigning large hill jumping champ from 1989,
Jim as the newly crowned normal hill champ for 1990, and Joe as reigning nordic
combined champion from 1989.

Parmesan Chicken and Pasta Salad

3 chicken breast fillets

1¹/₂ teaspoons vegetable oil

Crazy Salt, Italian seasoning, garlic powder and basil to taste

1 (16-ounce) package tri-colored rotini, cooked

1 cup mixed chopped green, red and yellow bell pepper

1 (4-ounce) jar sliced mushrooms, drained

3 tomatoes, coarsely chopped

1 (4-ounce) can sliced black olives, drained

1 (8-ounce) bottle Italian salad dressing

¹/₄ cup grated Parmesan cheese

* Cut the chicken into strips; rinse and pat dry.
* Sauté the chicken in the oil in a skillet. Season with Crazy Salt, Italian seasoning, garlic powder and basil.
* Combine the chicken, pasta, bell pepper, mushrooms, tomatoes and olives in a bowl. Add the salad dressing, tossing to coat well. Sprinkle with the cheese.
* Chill, covered, overnight.

Yield: 8 servings

Approx Per Serving: Cal 449; Prot 20 g; Carbo 50 g; T Fat 19 g;
38% Calories from Fat; Chol 30 mg; Fiber 3 g; Sod 465 mg

Lars Haugen (Minneapolis, MN) won seven U.S. ski jumping titles between 1912

and 1928. Jim Holland (Norwich, VT) won six between 1990 and 1993.

❄ Favorite Macaroni and Cheese ❄

6 cups water

1 (7-ounce) package macaroni and cheese dinner

$1/_4$ cup margarine

$1/_4$ cup milk

* Bring the water to a boil in a large saucepan. Add the macaroni.
* Boil for 7 to 10 minutes or until tender. Drain the macaroni and return to the saucepan.
* Add the margarine and milk and mix well. Add the cheese sauce and mix well.
* Serve with a fine chianti.

Yield: 3 servings

Approx Per Serving: Cal 394; Prot 11 g; Carbo 46 g; T Fat 18 g;
42% Calories from Fat; Chol 12 mg; Fiber 1 g; Sod 718 mg

Trace Worthington

World champion aerialist Trace ("The Ace") Worthington climbed previously unscaled heights
in 1995 when he won both the World Cup and World Championship aerials and combined titles. Now he
will chase Olympic gold in the 1998 Olympics in Nagano, Japan. Trace resides in Park City, Utah.

Nordic Combined Skiing

Nordic combined skiing, as the name implies, combines the two main elements of nordic skiing: cross country and jumping. Traditionally, it's a 90-meter jumping competition followed by a 15-kilometer ski race.

It's been called "the decathlon of skiing" because of the way it requires a skier to use two totally opposite muscle groups: explosiveness and strength for takeoff in jumping and then swiftness and endurance for cross country. "It's a real bear but it's fun, too," said Tim Tetreault, a two-time Olympian who switched to combined after several years of alpine racing and then "just" ski jumping.

Some observers have derided nordic combined athletes as not good enough to make it in either sport, jumping or ski-running. The reality is athletes have to master two sports to be good combined skiers.

For years, nordic combined was a two-day event, and it still is in many places. However, the World Cup tour has found that it's most spectator-friendly to sometimes stage one-day combined events. Skiers jump in the morning and race in the afternoon, or maybe it's a morning jump and a 15-km race under the lights at night.

Whether it's one day, though, or two, the format is the same: the top jumper goes first and, using the Gundersen handicap formula, is pursued by the rest of the field, according to the way they jumped, and the first skier to cross the finish wins.

While nordic combined—which, unlike cross country or jumping, remains an all-male sport—means getting hold of two sports, it also means an athlete doesn't have all his eggs in one basket. If he jumps poorly, there's always the chance to do well in the cross country race; if he jumps well, he's more than halfway home.

nd Side Dishes

Asparagus with Sesame Seeds

1½ pounds asparagus

1½ teaspoons unsalted margarine

1 tablespoon sesame seeds

1 teaspoon reduced-sodium soy sauce

1 teaspoon sesame oil

⅛ teaspoon pepper

* Rinse the asparagus; remove tough stems. Cut into 1-inch lengths.
* Fill a 10-inch skillet with 1 inch water. Bring to a boil.
* Add the asparagus. Cook, covered, for 3 minutes or until tender-crisp. Drain and rinse under cold running water. Drain and set aside.
* Melt the margarine in the skillet over medium heat. Add the sesame seeds.
* Sauté for 3 to 4 minutes or until golden brown.
* Return the asparagus to the skillet. Add the soy sauce, sesame oil and pepper.
* Cook for 1 minute or until heated through, stirring constantly.

Yield: 4 servings

Approx Per Serving: Cal 75; Prot 6 g; Carbo 7 g; T Fat 4 g;
43% Calories from Fat; Chol 0 mg; Fiber 3 g; Sod 68 mg

Only two U.S. skiers have won the Kings Cup, presented for winning the nordic

combined event at the Holmenkollen Ski Festival each year in Oslo, Norway. John Bower

(Auburn, ME) won in 1968 and Kerry Lynch (Silver Creek, CO) won in 1983.

Saucy Red Beans and Rice

1 onion, chopped

¹/₂ cup sliced celery

1 cup chopped zucchini

¹/₈ teaspoon garlic powder

¹/₄ teaspoon oregano

¹/₄ teaspoon thyme

1 (16-ounce) can chopped tomatoes

1 (15-ounce) can kidney beans, drained

¹/₈ teaspoon red pepper

2 cups cooked unsalted rice

* Spray a skillet with nonstick cooking spray.
* Combine the onion and celery in the skillet.
* Cook, covered, over medium-low heat until tender, stirring occasionally.
* Add the zucchini, garlic powder, oregano and thyme.
* Cook, uncovered, for 5 minutes, stirring occasionally.
* Add the tomatoes, kidney beans and red pepper.
* Simmer, uncovered, for 20 minutes, stirring occasionally.
* Serve over ¹/₂-cup portions of rice.

Yield: 4 servings

Approx Per Serving: Cal 231; Prot 10 g; Carbo 47 g; T Fat 1 g;
4% Calories from Fat; Chol 0 mg; Fiber 8 g; Sod 549 mg

Triple Bean Casserole

1 (16-ounce) can lima beans, drained

1 (31-ounce) can pork and beans in sauce

1 (15-ounce) can red kidney beans, drained

1 large onion, chopped

1 (7¹/₂-ounce) can tomatoes, chopped

¹/₄ cup packed brown sugar

1 tablespoon Worcestershire sauce

¹/₂ teaspoon dry mustard

¹/₂ cup bacon bits

* Combine the beans, onion, tomatoes, brown sugar, Worcestershire sauce, mustard and bacon bits in a bowl and mix well. Spoon into a 2-quart casserole.
* Bake, covered, at 375 degrees for 40 minutes. Bake, uncovered, for 25 to 30 minutes longer or until of the desired consistency.
* Serve hot or cold.

Yield: 20 servings

Approx Per Serving: Cal 124; Prot 6 g; Carbo 23 g; T Fat 2 g;
11% Calories from Fat; Chol 3 mg; Fiber 7 g; Sod 294 mg

Carrot and Rice Ring

3 cups cooked rice

2 cups grated carrots

1/4 cup grated onion

2 tablespoons flour

1 (10-ounce) can Cheddar cheese soup

1 egg, lightly beaten

1 teaspoon salt

1/4 teaspoon pepper

1 teaspoon Worcestershire sauce

1/8 teaspoon red hot sauce, or to taste

1 (10-ounce) package frozen peas

* Combine the rice, carrots, onion and flour in a large bowl. Add the soup, egg, salt, pepper, Worcestershire sauce and hot sauce and mix well.
* Press the mixture into a greased 8-inch ring mold.
* Bake at 350 degrees for 30 minutes.
* Cook the peas using the package directions; drain. Season to taste.
* Invert the rice ring onto a platter. Fill the center with peas.

Yield: 6 servings

Approx Per Serving: Cal 252; Prot 8 g; Carbo 42 g; T Fat 6 g;
21% Calories from Fat; Chol 47 mg; Fiber 4 g; Sod 829 mg

All-American Eggplant Stacks

6 (¹/₄-inch) slices eggplant

2 teaspoons olive oil

¹/₃ cup plus 2 teaspoons part-skim milk ricotta cheese

¹/₂ ounce cooked smoked ham, chopped

2 tablespoons chopped fresh basil, or ¹/₂ teaspoon dried

¹/₈ teaspoon pepper

6 slices tomato

2 ounces mozzarella cheese, shredded

* Arrange the eggplant slices on a baking sheet sprayed with nonstick cooking spray.
* Brush the eggplant with half the olive oil.
* Broil 5 to 6 inches from the heat source for 2 to 3 minutes or until light brown. Turn the slices and brush with the remaining olive oil.
* Broil for 2 to 3 minutes longer or until light brown.
* Combine the ricotta cheese, ham, basil and pepper in a bowl and mix well.
* Spread the cheese mixture on the eggplant slices. Top with the tomato slices. Sprinkle with the mozzarella cheese.
* Broil for 2 to 3 minutes or until the cheese melts.
* Let stand for 2 to 3 minutes before serving.

Yield: 2 servings

Approx Per Serving: Cal 253; Prot 14 g; Carbo 17 g; T Fat 15 g;
52% Calories from Fat; Chol 40 mg; Fiber 6 g; Sod 266 mg

Fiery Hopping John

1¹/₂ cups uncooked brown rice
¹/₂ cup dried black-eyed peas, cooked
1 large onion, chopped
3 jalapeños, finely chopped
3 cloves of garlic, minced
Salt to taste
4 cups shredded part-skim milk mozzarella cheese
4 ounces part-skim milk ricotta cheese
2 tablespoons 1% milk

* Cook the rice using the package directions.
* Combine the rice, black-eyed peas, onion, jalapeños, garlic and salt in a large bowl and mix well.
* Mix 3 cups of the mozzarella cheese, the ricotta cheese and milk in a medium bowl.
* Alternate layers of the rice mixture and cheese mixture in a 9x13-inch baking dish until all the ingredients are used, ending with the rice mixture.
* Bake at 350 degrees for 25 minutes.
* Sprinkle the remaining 1 cup mozzarella cheese over the top layer.
* Bake for 5 minutes longer.

Yield: 12 servings

Approx Per Serving: Cal 208; Prot 13 g; Carbo 22 g; T Fat 7 g;
32% Calories from Fat; Chol 24 mg; Fiber 2 g; Sod 274 mg

Spicy Lentil Curry

1¹/₂ cups dried lentils

1 teaspoon cumin seeds

1 tablespoon canola oil

1 large onion, chopped

1 medium tomato, chopped

1 red hot chile pepper

1 tablespoon ginger

1 clove of garlic, minced

¹/₂ teaspoon turmeric

¹/₂ teaspoon salt

* Combine the lentils with water to cover in a large saucepan. Simmer, partially covered, over medium heat for 45 to 50 minutes, stirring occasionally. Skim off the foam. Set aside.
* Sauté the cumin seeds in hot oil in a skillet for 1 minute. Add the onion. Cook for 4 to 5 minutes longer or until golden brown. Add the tomato and red pepper. Cook for 5 minutes longer or until the tomato is soft, stirring frequently. Remove the pepper.
* Add the tomato mixture, ginger, garlic, turmeric and salt to the lentils. Cook for 10 to 15 minutes longer or until heated through.
* Garnish with a dollop of yogurt. Serve with brown rice.

Yield: 6 servings

Approx Per Serving: Cal 201; Prot 14 g; Carbo 32 g; T Fat 3 g;
13% Calories from Fat; Chol 0 mg; Fiber 7 g; Sod 185 mg

Couscous with Roasted Red Peppers and Peas

6 to 8 shallots, sliced lengthwise
1 teaspoon canola oil
2 cups homemade chicken stock, fat skimmed
1¼ cups water
1 (10-ounce) package frozen green peas
1 cup coarsely chopped canned roasted red peppers, rinsed
1½ cups whole wheat couscous

* Sauté the shallots in the canola oil in a nonstick wok until tender. Add the chicken stock and water and mix well.
* Bring to a simmer. Stir in the peas.
* Simmer for 3 to 4 minutes or until the peas are tender-crisp. Add the red peppers and couscous.
* Simmer for 4 to 5 minutes. Remove from the heat.
* Let stand for 5 minutes.
* Prepare homemade chicken stock by bringing 3 chopped chicken legs and enough water to cover to a boil in a stockpot; discard the water and rinse the stockpot. Combine the chicken with 4 quarts water, 2 large onions, 2 carrots, celery and celery leaves. Bring to a boil; reduce the heat. Simmer for 2½ hours. Let cool. Strain the stock. Chill for 8 to 10 hours. Skim off any fat. May freeze for future use.

Yield: 4 servings

Approx Per Serving: Cal 422; Prot 18 g; Carbo 84 g; T Fat 3 g;
6% Calories from Fat; Chol 0 mg; Fiber 7 g; Sod 891 mg

Perfect-Edge Potatoes

6 large onions

7 pounds potatoes

Salt and pepper to taste

6 tablespoons vegetable oil

1 cup water

1¹/₂ pounds Cheddar cheese, sliced

* Slice the onions and potatoes ¹/₈ inch thick.
* Cover the bottom of a Dutch oven with onions. Sprinkle with salt and pepper. Place a 1-inch layer of potatoes on top.
* Repeat the layers until the Dutch oven is filled, seasoning layers with salt and pepper.
* Pour 1¹/₂ tablespoons of the oil in each corner of the Dutch oven. Add the water and cover. Place over medium-hot coals.
* Cook for 45 minutes or until the potatoes are tender.
* Top with the cheese. Cook just until the cheese melts.

Yield: 20 servings

Approx Per Serving: Cal 352; Prot 12 g; Carbo 44 g; T Fat 15 g;
38% Calories from Fat; Chol 32 mg; Fiber 4 g; Sod 500 mg

Nordic combined skier Ryan Heckman (Steamboat Springs, CO) holds a U.S. record which probably never will be broken: six years on the U.S. Ski Team and six major championships—the 1992 and 1994 Olympics, the 1991, 1993, 1995, and 1997 World Championships.

Squash and Corn Casserole

7 medium yellow squash

1 onion, chopped

1 green bell pepper, chopped

2 tablespoons butter

2 cups whole kernel corn

1 egg, beaten

¹/₄ cup melted butter

Salt and pepper to taste

1 cup (about) butter cracker crumbs

* Cut the squash into pieces. Combine with a small amount of water in a saucepan. Cook until tender; drain.
* Sauté the onion and green pepper in 2 tablespoons butter in a skillet until light brown.
* Combine the squash, sautéed vegetables and corn in a large bowl. Add the egg, melted butter, salt and pepper and mix well. Pour into a buttered baking dish. Sprinkle with the cracker crumbs.
* Bake at 350 degrees for 1 hour or until firm.

Yield: 10 servings

Approx Per Serving: Cal 174; Prot 5 g; Carbo 20 g; T Fat 10 g;
48% Calories from Fat; Chol 40 mg; Fiber 4 g; Sod 146 mg

Glazed Sweet Potatoes

4 large sweet potatoes

1 (8-ounce) can crushed pineapple

³/4 cup packed brown sugar

¹/4 teaspoon salt

1¹/2 tablespoons cornstarch

¹/8 teaspoon cinnamon

2 teaspoons grated orange peel

1 cup undrained canned apricots, puréed

2 tablespoons butter, softened

¹/2 cup chopped pecans

* Cook the sweet potatoes in water to cover in a saucepan until tender; drain. Cool to room temperature.
* Peel the sweet potatoes and cut into ¹/2-inch slices.
* Layer the sweet potatoes in a greased 8x13-inch baking dish.
* Drain the pineapple, reserving ¹/3 cup syrup. Combine the reserved syrup, brown sugar, salt, cornstarch, cinnamon, orange peel and apricot purée in a saucepan. Cook until thickened, stirring constantly.
* Add the butter, pecans and pineapple and mix well. Pour over the sweet potatoes.
* Bake at 375 degrees for 20 minutes or until heated through and bubbly.

Yield: 8 servings

Approx Per Serving: Cal 322; Prot 2 g; Carbo 63 g; T Fat 8 g;
22% Calories from Fat; Chol 8 mg; Fiber 4 g; Sod 114 mg

Cheesy Vegetable Rice

1/4 cup chopped onion

3 tablespoons butter

1 1/2 cups sliced mushrooms

2 cups chopped broccoli

1 cup chopped tomato

2 cups water

2 chicken bouillon cubes

1 cup uncooked rice

1/2 teaspoon salt

1/2 teaspoon oregano

1/4 cup grated Parmesan cheese

* Sauté the onion in the butter in a skillet until golden brown. Add the mushrooms, broccoli and tomato. Cook for 4 minutes, stirring frequently.
* Add the water and bouillon cubes. Bring to a boil.
* Stir in the rice, salt and oregano. Cook, covered, over low heat for 20 minutes or until the water is absorbed. Mix in the cheese.
* Serve hot or cold.

Yield: 6 servings

Approx Per Serving: Cal 204; Prot 5 g; Carbo 30 g; T Fat 7 g;
31% Calories from Fat; Chol 18 mg; Fiber 2 g; Sod 686 mg

Golden Vegetable Bake

4 cups chopped cauliflower

1 (10-ounce) package frozen brussels sprouts

$1/2$ teaspoon sugar

$1/4$ teaspoon rosemary

$1/2$ teaspoon celery salt

$3/4$ cup shredded Swiss cheese

2 egg whites

2 egg yolks

2 teaspoons milk

$1/8$ teaspoon salt

$1/8$ teaspoon pepper

2 tablespoons grated Parmesan cheese

* Combine the cauliflower with water to cover in a medium saucepan. Bring to a boil; reduce the heat.
* Simmer, covered, for 5 to 10 minutes or until tender; drain.
* Combine the cauliflower, brussels sprouts, sugar, rosemary and celery salt in a bowl and mix well. Spoon into a greased $1^1/2$-quart baking dish. Sprinkle with the Swiss cheese.
* Beat the egg whites in a mixer bowl until stiff peaks form.
* Beat the egg yolks with the milk, salt and pepper in a bowl until thick and pale yellow. Fold the beaten egg yolks and Parmesan cheese into the egg whites. Spread over the vegetable mixture.
* Bake at 350 degrees for 15 minutes or until golden brown.

Yield: 8 servings

Approx Per Serving: Cal 94; Prot 7 g; Carbo 6 g; T Fat 5 g;
48% Calories from Fat; Chol 64 mg; Fiber 3 g; Sod 248 mg

Low-Fat Veggie Bundles

1 large purple onion, cut into 4 slices

4 yellow squash, sliced

1 large tomato, cut into 4 slices

1 stalk broccoli, cut into florets

1/4 cup balsamic vinegar

2 tablespoons Champagne mustard

Sprig of fresh rosemary or tarragon

Fresh peppercorns

* Spray four 12x20-inch sheets of foil with nonstick cooking spray.
* Place 1 onion slice in the center of each piece of foil. Add a layer of squash, tomato and broccoli. Pour a mixture of the vinegar and mustard over the layers. Cut the rosemary and grind the pepper over the top. Seal the foil.
* Place the bundles on a baking sheet.
* Bake at 400 degrees for 20 minutes.
* Serve individually or place on a serving platter.

Yield: 4 servings

Approx Per Serving: Cal 106; Prot 0 g; Carbo 22 g; T Fat 1 g;
8% Calories from Fat; Chol 0 mg; Fiber 7 g; Sod 132 mg

Snowboarding

Snowboarding, like cross country skiing (with classical or freestyle technique), has two distinct elements: alpine and freestyle. And, like cross country's "mixed" relay format with classic and freestyle techniques, there's boardercross, which mixes alpine and freestyle in a follow-the-leader, beat-the-leader slice of downhill pandemonium.

One main difference between skiing and snowboarding is the start. Although skiers and riders break a wand to start their clock running, snowboarders use posts (usually 2x2-inch boards) driven into the snow to push off.

Like the competetive skiing it's derived from, alpine snowboarding has "technical" events (gate-running, slalom/giant slalom) and speed racing (super G). It's a beat-the-clock format—no judging, just be the fastest one down the course. Unlike World Cup alpine skiing, snowboarding also has a parallel slalom race with riders competing on side-by-side courses.

Parallel slalom uses a knockout format to determine the winner. Riders are timed in a qualifying run; based on their time, the men's field is cut to 16 and the women's field is reduced to eight. At that point, it's total time from one run on a blue course and one on a red course deciding who moves to the next round.

In freestyle, riders perform in a halfpipe, a giant snow trough, with competitors performing various tricks while three or five judges grade their acrobatic maneuvers (rotations, standard maneuvers, landings, technical merit, and amplitude).

Boardercross (or "snowboardercross") is the second new World Cup discipline. Depending on the number of participants in a race, four or six riders are at the starting line together, and simultaneously ride down a slope studded with various obstacles (i.e., moguls, steeps, jumps, waves). The two or three competitors who cross the finish line first qualify for the next round of competition in this elimination-format event.

Desserts

Baked Apple Dumplings with Lemon Sauce

2 cups baking mix

1 tablespoon vegetable oil

¹/₂ cup ice water

7 medium apples, peeled, cored

7 teaspoons butter, softened

¹/₂ cup packed brown sugar

1¹/₂ teaspoons cinnamon

1 cup sugar

2 cups water

¹/₂ teaspoon cornstarch

1 tablespoon butter

1 tablespoon lemon extract

* Combine the baking mix, oil and ¹/₂ cup ice water in a bowl and mix well.
* Roll ¹/₄ inch thick on a lightly floured surface. Cut into 7 squares.
* Place 1 apple on each square. Fill the apples with softened butter and a mixture of brown sugar and cinnamon.
* Bring up the corners of the dough to enclose the apples; secure with wooden picks.
* Place the apples in a greased 10x10-inch baking dish.
* Bring the sugar and 1¹/₂ cups of the 2 cups water to a boil in a saucepan. Blend the remaining ¹/₂ cup water with the cornstarch. Add to the boiling syrup.
* Cook until thickened, stirring constantly. Stir in 1 tablespoon butter and lemon extract. Pour over the dumplings.
* Bake at 350 degrees for 1 hour.

Yield: 7 servings

Approx Per Serving: Cal 403; Prot 2 g; Carbo 80 g; T Fat 10 g;
35% Calories from Fat; Chol 15 mg; Fiber 3 g; Sod 274 mg

Cherry Cobbler

1/2 cup shortening

1 cup sugar

1 cup milk

1 1/2 cups flour

2 teaspoons baking powder

1/2 teaspoon salt

2 cups cherries

1 cup sugar

1 1/2 cups boiling water

2 tablespoons butter

* Cream the shortening and 1 cup sugar in a mixer bowl until light and fluffy.
* Add the milk and mix well.
* Beat in the flour, baking powder and salt until smooth.
* Spread in a 9x13-inch baking dish.
* Top with the cherries. Sprinkle with 1 cup sugar.
* Pour the boiling water over the prepared layers. Dot with the butter.
* Bake at 350 degrees for 45 minutes.

Yield: 10 servings

Approx Per Serving: Cal 371; Prot 3 g; Carbo 60 g; T Fat 14 g;
33% Calories from Fat; Chol 10 mg; Fiber 1 g; Sod 208 mg

Chocolate Fudge Upside-Down Dessert

1 cup flour

1/4 teaspoon salt

1 teaspoon baking powder

1 1/2 tablespoons baking cocoa

3/4 cup sugar

1 tablespoon butter, softened

1/2 cup milk

1/2 cup chopped walnuts

1/2 cup sugar

1/2 cup packed brown sugar

1/4 cup baking cocoa

1 1/4 cups boiling water

* Sift the flour, salt, baking powder and 1 1/2 tablespoons cocoa together.
* Cream 3/4 cup sugar and butter in a mixer bowl until light and fluffy. Stir in the milk. Add the flour mixture and mix well.
* Spread in a buttered 9x9-inch baking pan. Sprinkle with the walnuts. Sprinkle with a mixture of 1/2 cup sugar, brown sugar and 1/4 cup baking cocoa.
* Pour the boiling water over the top; do not stir.
* Bake at 350 degrees for 45 minutes. Let stand until cool.
* Serve upside down with whipped topping.

Yield: 6 servings

Approx Per Serving: Cal 400; Prot 5 g; Carbo 78 g; T Fat 10 g;
21% Calories from Fat; Chol 8 mg; Fiber 3 g; Sod 182 mg

Warm Gingered Compote

1 (16-ounce) can juice-pack cling peach slices

1 (16-ounce) can juice-pack Bartlett pear halves

³/4 cup apple juice

1 teaspoon lemon juice

1 teaspoon grated lemon peel

¹/2 teaspoon ground ginger

¹/2 cup dried apricots

¹/4 cup currants

1 (16-ounce) can juice-pack chunky fruit, drained

* Drain the peaches and pears, reserving the juice.
* Combine the reserved juice, apple juice, lemon juice, lemon peel and ginger in a saucepan. Simmer for 15 minutes.
* Stir in the apricots and currants. Simmer for 10 minutes longer. Let stand until cooled to room temperature.
* Stir in the peaches, pears and chunky fruit.
* Store in the refrigerator. Reheat to serve.

Yield: 6 servings

Approx Per Serving: Cal 163; Prot 2 g; Carbo 42 g; T Fat <1 g;
0% Calories from Fat; Chol 0 mg; Fiber 4 g; Sod 12 mg

Sabrina Sadeghi (Aspen, CO) didn't just win the inaugural FIS World Cup title in halfpipe during the 1994-95 season, she was one of the top gate-running snowboarders; in 1997, she won the gold medal in giant slalom at the 1997 World Championships in San Candido, Italy.

Lemon Snow

2 envelopes unflavored gelatin

$^1/_2$ cup cold water

$^1/_2$ cup boiling water

1 cup sugar

2 cups ice water

$^3/_4$ cup lemon juice

1 tablespoon grated lemon peel

4 egg whites, stiffly beaten

1 tablespoon cornstarch

$^1/_2$ cup sugar

$^1/_4$ teaspoon salt

1 cup water

1 teaspoon grated lemon peel

3 tablespoons lemon juice

1 tablespoon butter or margarine

* Soften the gelatin in $^1/_2$ cup cold water in a double boiler. Stir in $^1/_2$ cup boiling water.
* Cook over low heat until the gelatin is dissolved, stirring constantly.
* Add 1 cup sugar. Cook until dissolved, stirring constantly. Remove from the heat.
* Add the ice water, $^3/_4$ cup lemon juice and 1 tablespoon lemon peel and mix well.
* Let stand until partially set. Beat until frothy. Fold in the egg whites.
* Chill for 2 to 4 hours.
* Combine the cornstarch, $^1/_2$ cup sugar, salt and 1 cup water in a saucepan. Add 1 teaspoon lemon peel, 3 tablespoons lemon juice and butter and mix well. Bring to a boil, stirring constantly until smooth. Let stand until cool.
* Spoon Lemon Snow into dessert bowls. Drizzle with the lemon sauce.

Yield: 8 servings

Approx Per Serving: Cal 183; Prot 3 g; Carbo 41 g; T Fat 1 g;
7% Calories from Fat; Chol 4 mg; Fiber <1 g; Sod 113 mg

Neapolitans

8 ounces almond paste

1 cup sugar

4 egg yolks

1¹/₂ cups butter, softened

1 teaspoon almond or vanilla extract

2 cups flour

4 egg whites, stiffly beaten

8 drops of red food coloring

8 drops of green food coloring

1 (10-ounce) jar seedless raspberry jam

1 (10-ounce) jar apricot preserves

3 cups semisweet chocolate chips

* Grease the bottoms and sides of three 9x13-inch baking pans. Line each with greased waxed paper.
* Break up the almond paste in a large mixer bowl. Add the sugar, egg yolks, butter and almond flavoring. Beat for 5 minutes or until fluffy.
* Beat in the flour. Fold in the egg whites.
* Divide the batter into 3 equal portions. Add red coloring to 1 batch, green coloring to 1 batch and leave 1 batch plain. Spread a different color batter in each prepared pan.
* Bake at 350 degrees for 10 minutes or until the edges begin to brown. Remove from the pans and invert onto wire racks. Remove the waxed paper. Cool the layers thoroughly.
* Place 1 layer on a baking sheet. Spread with the jam. Top with the second layer. Spread with the preserves. Top with the third layer.
* Cover with plastic wrap and weight with books. Store in a cool place for several hours or overnight.
* Trim and discard the brown edges.
* Melt the chocolate chips in a saucepan. Spread over the top layer.
* Dry for 30 minutes or longer before cutting into bars.

Yield: 48 servings

Approx Per Serving: Cal 193; Prot 0 g; Carbo 25 g; T Fat 11 g;
51% Calories from Fat; Chol 33 mg; Fiber 2 g; Sod 70 mg

Peach Meringue with Raspberries

4 fresh peaches

3 egg whites

1 tablespoon honey, warmed

2 (10-ounce) packages frozen unsweetened raspberries, thawed

* Peel the peaches and cut into halves. Place cut side up in a greased shallow baking dish.
* Beat the egg whites until soft peaks form. Add the honey gradually, beating constantly until stiff peaks form. Spoon into the center of each peach.
* Bake at 450 degrees for 4 to 5 minutes or until light brown.
* Spread the raspberries in a large flat serving dish. Arrange the peach halves in the raspberries.
* May substitute one 29-ounce can peaches, drained, for fresh peaches.

Yield: 8 servings

Approx Per Serving: Cal 105; Prot 2 g; Carbo 26 g; T Fat <1 g;
1% Calories from Fat; Chol 0 mg; Fiber 4 g; Sod 20 mg

Ross Powers (S. Londonderry, VT) led a 1-2-3 sweep by U.S. riders in halfpipe at the first FIS World Snowboard Championships in 1996. Powers took the gold with Lael Gregory (Eugene, OR) picking up silver and Rob Kingwill (Jackson, WY) taking home the bronze from Lienz, Austria.

Wine-Poached Pears

6 firm medium or large Bartlett pears
1³/₄ cups dry red wine
1 cup sugar
¹/₄ teaspoon anise seeds
2 whole cinnamon sticks
2 or 3 lemon slices

* Remove the core from the bottom end of each pear, leaving the stems in place. Peel the pears if desired.
* Combine the wine, sugar, anise seeds, cinnamon sticks and lemon slices in a pan large enough to hold the pears side by side. Bring the mixture to a boil over high heat.
* Arrange the pears side by side in the boiling mixture; reduce the heat to medium. Simmer, covered, for 8 to 10 minutes or until the pears are heated through but still firm, turning the pears occasionally.
* Remove the pears with a slotted spoon to a serving dish.
* Boil the syrup over high heat until reduced to ³/₄ to 1 cup. Pour over and around the pears.
* Serve warm or at room temperature.

Yield: 6 servings

Approx Per Serving: Cal 303; Prot 1 g; Carbo 66 g; T Fat 1 g;
2% Calories from Fat; Chol 0 mg; Fiber 6 g; Sod 4 mg

Pineapple Mint Frozen Yogurt

1 (8-ounce) can juice-pack crushed pineapple
1 cup plain yogurt
1/3 cup apple juice concentrate
1 1/2 teaspoons lemon juice
1/2 teaspoon vanilla extract
1/8 teaspoon salt
1/4 teaspoon mint extract
4 to 6 drops of green food coloring

* Drain the pineapple, reserving the juice.
* Combine the reserved juice, yogurt, apple juice concentrate and lemon juice in a saucepan. Cook over low heat for 2 to 3 minutes or until the yogurt dissolves, stirring frequently.
* Let stand until cool. Pour the cooled mixture into a mixer bowl.
* Add the pineapple, vanilla, salt, mint extract and food coloring and mix well. Pour into a freezer tray.
* Freeze until very thick but not hard. Place in a mixer bowl. Beat until smooth and fluffy. Pour into a covered freezer container.
* Freeze, covered, for 4 hours or until firm.
* Let stand at room temperature for 10 minutes before serving.

Yield: 5 servings

Approx Per Serving: Cal 88; Prot 2 g; Carbo 17 g; T Fat 2 g;
16% Calories from Fat; Chol 6 mg; Fiber 1 g; Sod 79 mg

Mike Jacoby (Hood River, OR) was the No. 1 giant slalom rider during the first two seasons
of the FIS World Cup tour. Jacoby was the men's giant slalom champion in those first two seasons, not
including a silver medal in giant slalom (behind teammate Jeff Greenwood of Granby, CT) at the 1996
World Championships. Jacoby also won the GS silver at the 1997 Worlds in San Candido, Italy.

Sugar-Free Pumpkin Chiffon Dessert

2 envelopes unflavored gelatin

1/2 cup cold water

1 cup flour

1/2 cup chopped pecans

1/4 cup melted margarine

6 egg yolks, beaten

2 (16-ounce) cans unsweetened pumpkin

2 teaspoons cinnamon

1 teaspoon nutmeg

2 teaspoons ginger

2 cups skim milk

6 egg whites, chilled

1/2 teaspoon cream of tartar

18 to 20 envelopes artificial sweetener

* Soften the gelatin in cold water and mix well.
* Combine the flour, pecans and margarine in a bowl and mix well. Press over the bottom and 1/4 inch up the side of a 9-inch springform pan.
* Bake at 350 degrees for 15 minutes. Let stand until cool.
* Combine the egg yolks, pumpkin, cinnamon, nutmeg, ginger and skim milk in a saucepan and mix well. Bring to a boil over low heat, stirring constantly. Cook for 2 minutes, stirring constantly.
* Stir in the gelatin. Cook until the gelatin dissolves, stirring constantly. Let stand until cool.
* Beat the egg whites in a mixer bowl until soft peaks form. Add the cream of tartar and artificial sweetener, beating constantly until stiff peaks form.
* Fold into the pumpkin mixture. Spread over the baked layer.
* Chill until set.
* Garnish with sugar-free whipped topping.
* May add 1 teaspoon salt to the pumpkin mixture.

Yield: 12 servings

Approx Per Serving: Cal 211; Prot 8 g; Carbo 19 g; T Fat 12 g;
50% Calories from Fat; Chol 107 mg; Fiber 3 g; Sod 132 mg

Prize-Winning Chocolate Rice

2 cups rice

2 cups milk

1 teaspoon grated lemon peel

1 egg yolk

¹/₄ cup sugar

7 ounces unsweetened chocolate

1 teaspoon butter

1 egg white, stiffly beaten

¹/₄ cup fine bread crumbs

* Cook the rice in the milk in a saucepan using the package directions; strain.
* Combine the lemon peel, egg yolk and sugar in a bowl and mix well.
* Combine the chocolate and butter in a saucepan. Heat over medium heat until the chocolate melts, stirring occasionally. Remove from the heat.
* Add the chocolate to the egg yolk mixture and mix well. Combine the egg white and rice in a bowl and mix well. Add to the chocolate mixture and mix well.
* Grease a 2-quart baking dish with a tube center. Sprinkle with the bread crumbs. Pour in the chocolate mixture.
* Bake at 350 degrees for 30 to 45 minutes or until set.
* Cool on a wire rack. Invert onto a serving plate.
* Garnish with flavored whipped cream.

Yield: 8 servings

Approx Per Serving: Cal 382; Prot 9 g; Carbo 55 g; T Fat 17 g;
37% Calories from Fat; Chol 36 mg; Fiber 5 g; Sod 63 mg

Deluxe Applesauce Cake

³/₄ cup sifted flour
1 cup coarsely chopped walnuts
1 cup raisins
1 cup pitted dates, chopped
2 cups sifted flour
1 teaspoon salt
1 teaspoon cinnamon
1 teaspoon ground cloves
¹/₄ teaspoon ginger
1 (16-ounce) can applesauce
2 teaspoons baking soda
¹/₂ cup shortening
1 cup sugar

* Combine ³/₄ cup flour, walnuts, raisins and dates in a bowl, tossing to coat.
* Sift 2 cups flour, salt, cinnamon, cloves and ginger into a bowl and mix well.
* Combine the applesauce and baking soda in a bowl and mix well.
* Cream the shortening and sugar in a mixer bowl until light and fluffy. Add the sifted dry ingredients alternately with the applesauce mixture ¹/₃ at a time, beating well after each addition.
* Stir in the walnut mixture. Spoon into a greased tube pan.
* Bake at 350 degrees for 1 hour and 10 minutes.
* Invert onto a funnel to cool. Loosen the cake from the side of the pan. Invert onto a cake plate.
* Frost with your favorite mocha frosting.

Yield: 16 servings

Approx Per Serving: Cal 308; Prot 4 g; Carbo 51 g; T Fat 11 g;
32% Calories from Fat; Chol 0 mg; Fiber 3 g; Sod 240 mg

Boardercross Berry Torte

1 cup low-fat sour cream

1 egg, lightly beaten

2 tablespoons sugar

1 tablespoon plus 1 teaspoon lemon juice

1/4 teaspoon vanilla extract

1 (9-inch) graham cracker pie shell

1 cup sliced strawberries

1 cup blueberries or raspberries

2 or 3 kiwifruit, sliced

1/3 cup raspberry jam

Lemon juice or water to taste

* Whisk the sour cream, egg, sugar, lemon juice and vanilla together in a bowl. Pour into the pie shell.
* Bake at 325 degrees for 15 to 20 minutes or until set.
* Chill, covered, for 20 to 30 minutes.
* Arrange the strawberries around the outer edge of the torte. Place the blueberries in the center. Arrange the kiwifruit in between.
* Combine the jam and lemon juice in a saucepan and mix well. Cook until of honey consistency, stirring constantly. Brush over the fruit.
* Chill, covered, until serving time.
* May substitute fat-free sour cream for low-fat sour cream.

Yield: 8 servings

Approx Per Serving: Cal 329; Prot 4 g; Carbo 48 g; T Fat 15 g;
39% Calories from Fat; Chol 38 mg; Fiber 3 g; Sod 260 mg

Blueberry Kuchen

1 cup flour

2 tablespoons sugar

$^1/_4$ teaspoon salt

$^1/_2$ cup butter, softened

1 tablespoon white vinegar

2 tablespoons flour

1 cup sugar

$^1/_4$ teaspoon cinnamon

3 cups blueberries

Confectioners' sugar to taste

* Combine 1 cup flour, 2 tablespoons sugar and salt in a bowl and mix well. Cut in the butter with a pastry blender until crumbly. Stir in the vinegar. Press over the bottom and 1 inch up the side of a 9-inch springform pan.
* Combine 2 tablespoons flour, 1 cup sugar and cinnamon in a bowl. Fold in 2 cups of the blueberries. Spoon into the prepared pan.
* Bake at 400 degrees for 1 hour.
* Sprinkle with the remaining blueberries.
* Let stand until cool. Remove the side of the pan. Sprinkle with confectioners' sugar.
* May serve with whipped cream or ice cream.

Yield: 8 servings

Approx Per Serving: Cal 305; Prot 2 g; Carbo 49 g; T Fat 12 g;
34% Calories from Fat; Chol 31 mg; Fiber 2 g; Sod 188 mg

Hall of Fame Banana Pudding

5 cups cold milk

3 (4-ounce) packages vanilla instant pudding mix

12 ounces whipped topping

1 (16-ounce) container vanilla yogurt

1 (12-ounce) package vanilla wafers

6 or 7 ripe bananas, sliced

* Whisk the milk and pudding mix in a bowl. Whisk in the whipped topping and yogurt.
* Alternate layers of vanilla wafers, bananas and pudding in a large glass bowl, beginning with vanilla wafers and ending with pudding.
* Garnish with vanilla wafer crumbs.
* To reduce fat in this recipe, use skim or 1/2% milk, low-fat whipped topping and low-fat or fat-free yogurt. Sugar-free pudding mix may also be used.

Yield: 10 servings

Approx Per Serving: Cal 560; Prot 5 g; Carbo 91 g; T Fat 20 g;
32% Calories from Fat; Chol 41 mg; Fiber 2 g; Sod 632 mg

Old-Fashioned Rice Pudding

1/2 cup uncooked rice

1/2 cup sugar

1/2 teaspoon salt

1/2 teaspoon nutmeg

8 cups 1% milk

3/4 cup raisins

* Combine the rice, sugar, salt, nutmeg and milk in a bowl and mix well. Pour into a 2¹/₂-quart baking dish.
* Bake at 325 degrees for 1¹/₂ hours, stirring twice.
* Add the raisins. Bake for 1 hour or until brown.
* Serve warm or chilled.
* Do not use skim milk in this recipe; it will affect the consistency of the pudding. May omit the raisins.

Yield: 10 servings

Approx Per Serving: Cal 191; Prot 7 g; Carbo 36 g; T Fat 2 g;
10% Calories from Fat; Chol 8 mg; Fiber 1 g; Sod 207 mg

Equivalents

When the recipe calls for	*Use*
Baking	
$^1/_2$ cup butter	4 ounces
2 cups butter	1 pound
4 cups all-purpose flour	1 pound
$4^1/_2$ to 5 cups sifted cake flour	1 pound
1 square chocolate	1 ounce
1 cup semisweet chocolate chips	6 ounces
4 cups marshmallows	1 pound
$2^1/_4$ cups packed brown sugar	1 pound
4 cups confectioners' sugar	1 pound
2 cups granulated sugar	1 pound
Cereal & Bread	
1 cup fine dry bread crumbs	4 to 5 slices
1 cup soft bread crumbs	2 slices
1 cup small bread cubes	2 slices
1 cup fine cracker crumbs	28 saltines
1 cup fine graham cracker crumbs	15 crackers
1 cup vanilla wafer crumbs	22 wafers
1 cup crushed cornflakes	3 cups uncrushed
4 cups cooked macaroni	8 ounces uncooked
$3^1/_2$ cups cooked rice	1 cup uncooked
Dairy	
1 cup shredded cheese	4 ounces
1 cup cottage cheese	8 ounces
1 cup sour cream	8 ounces
1 cup whipped cream	$^1/_2$ cup heavy cream
$^2/_3$ cup evaporated milk	1 small can
$1^2/_3$ cups evaporated milk	1 (13-ounce) can
Fruit	
4 cups sliced or chopped apples	4 medium
1 cup mashed bananas	3 medium
$2^1/_2$ cups shredded coconut	8 ounces
4 cups cranberries	1 pound
1 cup pitted dates	1 (8-ounce) package
3 to 4 tablespoons lemon juice plus 1 tablespoon grated lemon peel	1 lemon
$^1/_3$ cup orange juice plus 2 teaspoons grated orange peel	1 orange
4 cups sliced peaches	8 medium
3 cups raisins	1 (15-ounce) package

Equivalents

When the recipe calls for	Use

Meats

4 cups chopped cooked chicken	1 (5-pound) chicken
3 cups chopped cooked meat	1 pound, cooked
2 cups cooked ground meat	1 pound, cooked

Nuts

1 cup chopped nuts	4 ounces shelled or 1 pound unshelled

Vegetables

2 cups cooked green beans	$^1/_2$ pound fresh or 1 (16-ounce) can
2$^1/_2$ cups lima beans or red beans	1 cup dried, cooked
4 cups shredded cabbage	1 pound
1 cup grated carrot	1 large
8 ounces fresh mushrooms	1 (4-ounce) can
1 cup chopped onion	1 large
4 cups sliced or chopped potatoes	4 medium
2 cups canned tomatoes	1 (16-ounce) can

Measurement Equivalents

1 tablespoon = 3 teaspoons
2 tablespoons = 1 ounce
4 tablespoons = $^1/_4$ cup
5$^1/_3$ tablespoons = $^1/_3$ cup
8 tablespoons = $^1/_2$ cup
12 tablespoons = $^3/_4$ cup
16 tablespoons = 1 cup
1 cup = 8 ounces or $^1/_2$ pint
4 cups = 1 quart
4 quarts = 1 gallon

1 (6$^1/_2$- to 8-ounce) can = 1 cup
1 (10$^1/_2$- to 12-ounce) can = 1$^1/_4$ cups
1 (14- to 16-ounce) can = 1$^3/_4$ cups
1 (16- to 17-ounce) can = 2 cups
1 (18- to 20-ounce) can = 2$^1/_2$ cups
1 (29-ounce) can = 3$^1/_2$ cups
1 (46- to 51-ounce) can = 5$^3/_4$ cups
1 (6$^1/_2$- to 7$^1/_2$-pound) can or
Number 10 = 12 to 13 cups

Metric Equivalents

Liquid
1 teaspoon = 5 milliliters
1 tablespoon = 15 milliliters
1 fluid ounce = 30 milliliters
1 cup = 250 milliliters
1 pint = 500 milliliters

Dry
1 quart = 1 liter
1 ounce = 30 grams
1 pound = 450 grams
2.2 pounds = 1 kilogram

Substitutions

Instead of	*Use*

Baking

1 teaspoon baking powder	$1/4$ teaspoon baking soda plus $1/2$ teaspoon cream of tartar
1 tablespoon cornstarch	2 tablespoons flour or 1 tablespoon tapioca
1 cup sifted all-purpose flour	1 cup plus 2 tablespoons sifted cake flour
1 cup sifted cake flour	1 cup minus 2 tablespoons sifted all-purpose flour

Bread Crumbs

1 cup dry bread crumbs	$3/4$ cup cracker crumbs

Dairy

1 cup buttermilk	1 cup sour milk or 1 cup yogurt
1 cup heavy cream	$3/4$ cup milk plus $1/3$ cup butter
1 cup light cream	$7/8$ cup skim milk plus 3 tablespoons butter
1 cup sour cream	$7/8$ cup sour milk plus 3 tablespoons butter
1 cup sour milk	1 cup milk plus 1 tablespoon vinegar or lemon juice or 1 cup buttermilk

Seasoning

1 teaspoon allspice	$1/2$ teaspoon cinnamon plus $1/8$ teaspoon cloves
1 cup catsup	1 cup tomato sauce plus $1/2$ cup sugar plus 2 tablespoons vinegar
1 clove of garlic	$1/8$ teaspoon garlic powder or $1/8$ teaspoon instant minced garlic or $3/4$ teaspoon garlic salt or 5 drops of liquid garlic
1 teaspoon Italian spice	$1/4$ teaspoon each oregano, basil, thyme, rosemary plus dash of cayenne
1 teaspoon lemon juice	$1/2$ teaspoon vinegar
1 tablespoon mustard	1 teaspoon dry mustard
1 medium onion	1 tablespoon dried minced onion or 1 teaspoon onion powder

Sweet

1 (1-ounce) square chocolate	$1/4$ cup baking cocoa plus 1 teaspoon shortening
$1^2/3$ ounces semisweet chocolate	1 ounce unsweetened chocolate plus 4 teaspoons granulated sugar
1 cup honey	1 to $1^1/4$ cups sugar plus $1/4$ cup liquid or 1 cup corn syrup or molasses
1 cup granulated sugar	1 cup packed brown sugar or 1 cup corn syrup, molasses or honey minus $1/4$ cup liquid

Index

Order Information

On Course: The U.S. Ski & Snowboard Teams' Cookbook
U.S. Ski Team Foundation
P.O. Box 100
Park City, Utah 84060

Please send _____ copies of *On Course*   @ $14.95 each $ _____

Shipping and handling   @ $4.95 each $ _____

Total $ _____

_____
Name

_____
Address

_____
City   State   Zip

Method of payment   ○ Check   ○ VISA

Make checks payable to U.S. Ski Team Foundation.
VISA is the preferred credit card of the U.S. Ski and Snowboard Teams.

_____
Card Number

_____
Expiration Date

_____
Signature

Photocopies of this order form will be accepted.